James Arnold Taylor

Published by You Me Go, Inc. 2013

JAT 365

365 Daily Inspirations
for the
Pursuit of Your Dreams

Adapted from the social media of
James Arnold Taylor

JAT 365

Published by You Me Go, Inc.

ISBN 978-1492329282

Cover and Interior Design by James Arnold Taylor
Photography by Kelsey Edwards kelseyedwardsphoto.com

For more information visit www.JamesArnoldTaylor.com

Follow James on Twitter and Instagram at: @JATactor
Or visit and "Like" his fan page on Facebook

To my fans,
your constant enthusiasm for my work
keeps me excited for the next day.

Introduction

"Wake up and dream! Dream bigger than your imagination can imagine... Then, pursue it!"
                                                                    -JAT

Thank you for purchasing my book!

As an independent publishing I am truly grateful for your trust in me; and it is my hope that the investment of your money and time in yourself through this daily reader will hopefully inspire you to reach new goals and endeavors.

For those of you that may not have any idea who I am, or why I see fit to try and inspire you, allow me to introduce myself... My name is James Arnold Taylor and I am, by trade a "Voice-Actor", meaning, that I use my voice to act in TV, movies, radio, internet, video games, and more. I've been the voice of iconic characters like Fred Flintstone, Leonardo the Ninja Turtle, Obi-Wan Kenobi, and even new favorites like Johnny Test and Ratchet from Ratchet & Clank. So, let's say you are watching your favorite show and a voice comes on saying... *"Stick around! There's more (insert your favorite show name here), coming up!!"* That would be me... The voice that says that... not the show. Or perhaps you are into video games and every time you defeat an opponent and win a level, your character yells something like, *"See ya!!"* again, that's me. I may be the voices in the cartoon you see as you surf through the channels, even the mascot for your favorite breakfast cereal... Just me in a little padded room talking to myself. That's the life of a voice-actor and if we do our jobs right, most people never even think we exist.

Voice-Acting has allowed me to achieve many of my dreams and goals in life; one of which is to inspire others to pursue their dreams and goals. I've been able to maintain a very loyal and truly awesome group of fans through social media and my personal website, www.JamesArnoldTaylor.com. The most popular social media for me is Facebook and Twitter, and it is on both that I have established a regular place to post my positive remarks and thoughts to inspire others. I see myself as an "Ambassador of Inspiration" and I have found that by staying positive and using social media to positively reach out to others, that the fruits have been many letters of thanks from people that applied said positivity to their lives and are now doing more due to a changed attitude.

In this book, you will find many of the quotes I have posted to both Facebook and Twitter since 2010, and some new insights as well. I've also added a chance to use this as you would an on-line resource by giving extra space at the bottom of each page to write your own thoughts or "Comments" to help you journal along with me through the year. Plus, I've added three words at the top of each page that can be checked off at different times of the day as you utilize the inspiration for that day.

The three words are: *Accept, Forward,* and *Practice*. Each has a circle next to it that you can fill in or check off as you do them. The first word, *Accept,* should be checked off after you've read the day's inspiration and accept it into your thoughts. By accepting this inspiration that means you have read it (perhaps more than once) and plan on using it as a tool in your day to stay focused and inspired on the positive aspects of your life. You are committing not just to yourself, but to me as well with this action, and sometimes it takes committing to others besides ourselves to truly get something done.

The next word, *Forward,* is checked off after you've found someone to share the day's thought with. You could read it to someone or even use your smart phone (if you have one) and snap a picture of the page (make sure it's clear enough to read the inspiration) and send it off to a friend or loved one that needs it that day. For us to bring about change in our lives for the positive, we should be ready to bring others into our commitments as well. So the act of "Forwarding" this will not only keep you accountable, it will hopefully inspire them, and perhaps even get them to want to get a copy and do it for themselves daily. That may sound like I'm just trying to sell books, but I actually really want you to be changing for the better, and trying new things and ways of encouraging each other to affect the world around you.

The last word is, *Practice.* Check this one off by putting what you've read into action and make a plan to practice it regularly. As a parent of a young child who loves learning, I find myself constantly telling her to practice what she's learned in order to keep it living within her. She loves to play the piano, and at times believes she can just sit down and play a concerto, but what she finds when she places her hands on the keys, if she didn't practice, is much more like a convulsion of noise. We must practice what we desire and what we want to become. Practice can truly make all the difference in developing positive skills in our lives. I know that in school they never wanted you to write in your books, but remember this one is actually yours! You either paid for it, or it was given to you as a gift and now you can do with it as you please... You can stick it on a shelf and never let it do it's job, you can read each one and hopefully say them to yourself throughout the day to keep you inspired, *or* you can use this like a manual to a better more positive life, and write *your* thoughts on what's in it. Circle things, cross out things, draw a happy face when it hits you the right way, whatever you like. It doesn't matter; it's your book! Think of the fun things you'll remember and find out about yourself when you look back at it. Or perhaps you'll want a second copy for the next year to create new notes and inspirations! (I know, there he goes again trying to sell more books!)

I find the books that inspire me the most I highlight and underline, circle, draw stars on paragraphs, bend a corner over on favorite pages for quick access, so when I flip through it later I can see what really made the biggest impact on me. I want this book to truly help you be inspired and to feel joy in your daily life. We are all created to do more than we are presently doing, even if we are quite successful, we are in need of growth and the only way to grow is to stretch. So stretch yourself in a very small way by committing to reading (and writing in) this book everyday for the next 365 days. You don't have to start it on January 1st, in fact, I've purposely set the pages up to reflect numbers rather than dates, so as to not create any one starting date, and to get you motivated to begin right now. The quotes are also very short, most only one or two sentences, which means you could say them to yourself throughout the day and begin to truly apply positive thought patterns to your life. I hope you do, and I sincerely hope you come away from this book with more energy and inspiration to live a life full of experiences and fulfilled dreams and goals. I believe each of us is living for a reason, and to accomplish specific things. You may be artistic or quiet and introverted, either way, you are here to affect the world around you and inspire not only yourself, but others.

The other thing to remember is, you're never alone in this. I am right there with you, writing, reading, and believing in a better life for both of us. As someone with a faith in something far greater than me, I am praying for every person that picks this book up and even considers it. My hope in life is to see people believe in the positive within themselves, and to make (as corny as it sounds) the world a better place when I leave it than when I first came into it. You can be inspired and achieve the goals you set out for yourself daily. You just have to commit to doing it and hopefully this book will be of some help to you! So good luck and again, many thanks! I believe we can start this now with the goal of finishing it 365 days later, having a more positive outlook and tools to help achieve that.

I'd also like to add that while this book is to encourage and inspire, it is not going to create your dreams and goals for you. Nor should it be thought of as something with a traditional beginning, middle, and end, where you start with no dream and by the end have a finished plan. This book is made to keep you going in the day in and day out building of thought patterns that create a positive outlook, and in turn help you realize the person you want to be through said positivity.   So think of it as daily maintenance for your dreams.   When you're feeling less than up to pursuing the positive, you can always turn to this and find a pep talk.

One last thing... As I mentioned, I have a faith in something greater than me, that being God. At times in this book I may reference prayer, or faith; that is in no way to make you feel you must believe the way I do. It is the way I think and live, and I will always be honest about that, and am always available to answer questions from anyone that asks with the right intent of knowing more about it, through the contact page on my website.   I hope if you don't believe the way I do, you will still find the book useful and an encouraging part of your quest to fulfill your dreams.

God bless,
James Arnold Taylor
September 2013

JAT 365

365 Daily Inspirations
for the
Pursuit of Your Dreams

This book and all the dreams in it belong to:

Day 1

Inspire: Believe...

You can accomplish at least one goal this week, that will begin a change in your life. Know what it is and seek ways to achieve it.

Respond: What's your current goal?

Day 2

Accept ● Forward ● Practice ●

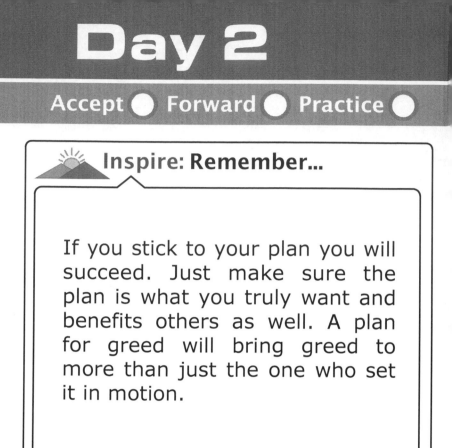

Inspire: Remember...

If you stick to your plan you will succeed. Just make sure the plan is what you truly want and benefits others as well. A plan for greed will bring greed to more than just the one who set it in motion.

Respond: Who benefits from your plan?

Day 3

Accept ● Forward ● Practice ●

 **Inspire: Know that...**

You are making a difference in others lives today, even if they don't tell you. Just you being you and present is different than life without you. Be the difference!

Respond: How do you make a difference?

Day 4

Inspire: No Fear...

For many of us the thing we fear is actually being happy and content with who we are. We are designed to love, not just others, but ourselves too. Reset your default to joy!

Respond: When do you feel happy?

Day 5

Accept ● Forward ● Practice ●

Inspire: You Can...

Throw away the negative and embrace joy! When the negative comes up, replace it with a positive thought, action, or deed that you could do or have done in the past. Practice this daily!

Respond: List some positives to use daily.

Day 6

Accept ● Forward ● Practice ●

Inspire: Know Inside...

We are all loved by someone. Friends, family, even people we may not realize. Take a moment to feel that love and give it back to them. Live in that love today.

Respond: Who loves you?

Day 7

Accept ● Forward ● Practice ●

 **Inspire: Seeking Quiet...**

Find a few minutes today to take some nice deep breaths and feel the silence and solitude of that moment. We can't rush all the time, it will catch up to us. Let the franticness fade.

Respond: Set a time & place for this today.

Day 8

Accept ● Forward ● Practice ●

Inspire: Free Yourself...

Don't let frustration make the rules. Remind yourself regularly, if something is hard, it's probably worth learning and enduring. You are becoming stronger!

Respond: What challenges you?

Day 9

Accept ● Forward ● Practice ●

Inspire: Letting Go...

If something is worrying you right now, you're missing the joy of living in this day. Anxiety only feeds stress, it doesn't get rid of it. Give it up, and know you are more than your worries.

Respond: What can you replace it with?

Day 10

Inspire: Simple Peace...

Simplify your daily life, and allow the mind to de-clutter. Clean out the parts that only bring clamor and replace them with open space for fine tuning your goals and dreams.

Respond: What is cluttering your mind?

Day 11

Accept ● Forward ● Practice ●

 **Inspire: Right Now...**

There should be no, "Someday I will..." in your life. Today is the perfect day to start or finish a goal or dream. If you don't, how can others be motivated or inspired by you?

Respond: What is your "Someday"?

Day 12

Inspire: In This Moment...

Enjoy the fact that you are alive and that you can accomplish your goals as effectively as breathing... *IF,* you apply yourself and seek truth in all things!

Respond: What is truth to you?

Day 13

Inspire: Clean Up...

Hit the "delete button" on the negative thoughts that come in today, the same way you do with the "spam" in your e-mail box. They're both worthless!

Respond: What can you "delete" right now?

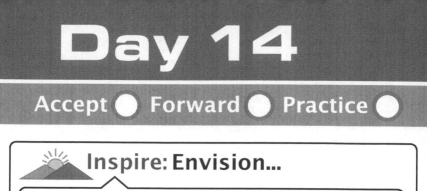

Accept ● Forward ● Practice ●

☀ Inspire: Envision...

Do you have a goal that you haven't achieved yet? How close are you, and what have you done today to bring yourself closer to it? Never let your dreams fade!

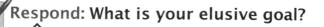

✎ Respond: What is your elusive goal?

Day 15

Inspire: Listen...

What are you hearing inside you? A voice that says, "You can!" or "You can't." Ask yourself, "Which is of worth to my success?" You CAN do it!

Respond: What do you want to tell you?

Day 16

Accept ● Forward ● Practice ●

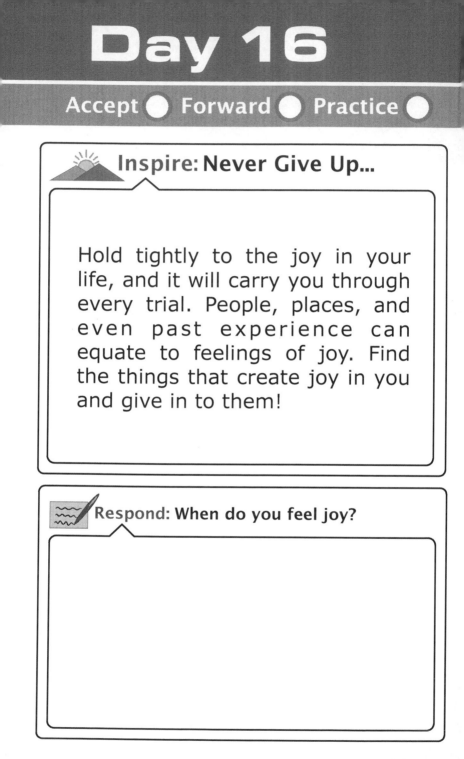

Inspire: Never Give Up...

Hold tightly to the joy in your life, and it will carry you through every trial. People, places, and even past experience can equate to feelings of joy. Find the things that create joy in you and give in to them!

Respond: When do you feel joy?

Day 17

Inspire: Name It...

If you can picture it in your mind, and it's good, it helps others, and brings you and them to a new place in life... Then, it's probably worth planning out and pursuing!

Respond: What's the "It" you want?

Day 18

Accept ● Forward ● Practice ●

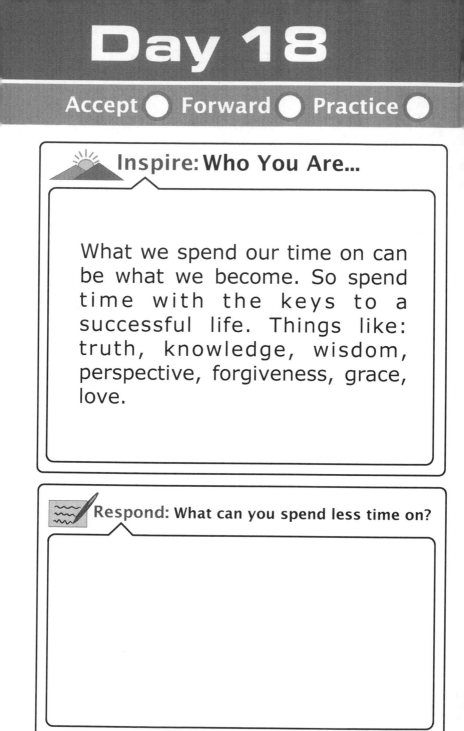

Inspire: Who You Are...

What we spend our time on can be what we become. So spend time with the keys to a successful life. Things like: truth, knowledge, wisdom, perspective, forgiveness, grace, love.

Respond: What can you spend less time on?

Day 19

Inspire: A Step Closer...

Put some time aside today to think about your dreams and then try a new way to go after them. A way you've never tried before and note what worked and what didn't. Then, see how much closer you are to achieving it.

Respond: List some new ways.

Day 20

Inspire: See Clearly...

Stay focused on your goals, and remind yourself daily of them. Tell yourself it's good to have them and that they will help you grow into the person you want to be!

Respond: Write down an encouragement.

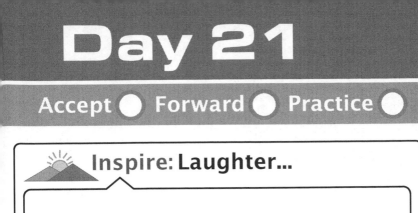

Day 21

Accept ● Forward ● Practice ●

Inspire: Laughter...

If you haven't yet today, find something that will make you laugh and give in to it! Laughter is good for your soul, feed it happiness and you will be happy!

Respond: What truly makes you laugh?

Day 22

Accept ● Forward ● Practice ●

Inspire: Thanksgiving...

It's great to be thankful, and to thank others for being in your life. Thank someone today for their encouragement and see how their kindness keeps you pressing forward!

Respond: List who you can thank today.

Day 23

Accept ● Forward ● Practice ●

Inspire: Want vs Need...

Think of the things that control you the most... The want of money, fame, recognition, love? Now, replace them with thoughts of doing for others, or what has been done for you... We are all crying out to be heard. Hear more than yourself and feel the weight of it.

Respond: What negatively controls you?

Day 24

Accept ● Forward ● Practice ●

Inspire: Just for You...

In case no one else has told you today, "You can do it!" Whatever it is that you've been struggling to overcome, or achieve, or simply believe in, you can do!

Respond: What would encourage you?

Day 25

Inspire: Past Hurts Heal...

All the things from your past happened to make you who you are right now, so even if they hurt, embrace them and take note. Don't look at it as punishment, look at it as strengthening.

Respond: What past hurt healed you?

Day 26

Inspire: Truth and Fear...

Look into the heart of what you fear most and tell it the truth... That it is a lie! Don't allow fear to control you in any part of your life!

Respond: List a fear and tell it the truth.

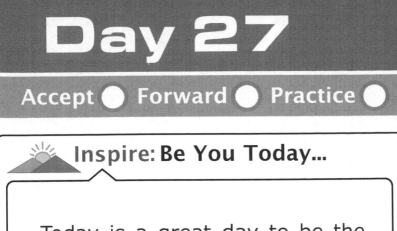

Day 27

Accept ● Forward ● Practice ●

Inspire: Be You Today...

Today is a great day to be the person you desire to be in life! Do your best to walk, talk, and act in every way as "You" perfected by truth. If you mess up, start over tomorrow, just like that "perfected you" would do!

Respond: What can you avoid being today?

Day 28

Accept ● Forward ● Practice ●

 **Inspire: Do What You Do...**

It's easier than you think to do what you do. The problem occurs when we think too much!

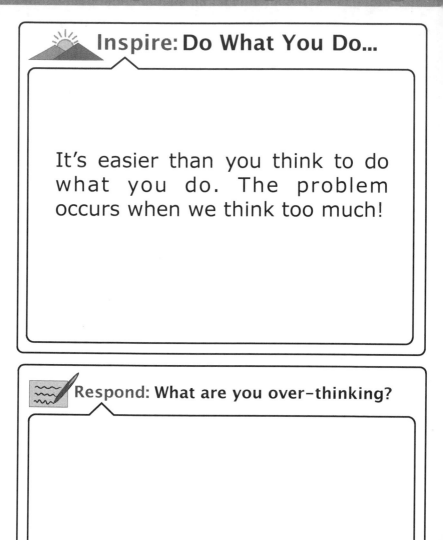 **Respond: What are you over-thinking?**

Day 29

Accept ● Forward ● Practice ●

 **Inspire: Tick, Tock...**

Time can be elusive, if we need it to be amounting to something other than it is... life! Simply live it and let it pass with ease.

Respond: What are you timing too much?

Day 30

 Inspire: Hope vs Despair...

For anyone that is losing hope today, know that hope is stronger than despair, because it never tries to be anything else. Despair lies about everything.

 Respond: What can you hope for today?

Day 31

Accept ● Forward ● Practice ●

☼ Inspire: Having Friends...

Relationships are so important to our life, not just to share with, but to listen to and through listening, receiving all the more.

Respond: Who are you listening to?

Day 32

Accept ● Forward ● Practice ●

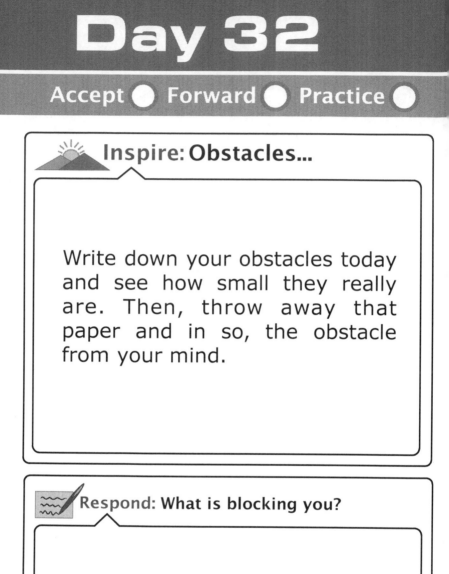

Inspire: Obstacles...

Write down your obstacles today and see how small they really are. Then, throw away that paper and in so, the obstacle from your mind.

Respond: What is blocking you?

Day 33

Inspire: Past Helps Future...

Take a moment and write down something you've accomplished in the past and remind yourself how you did it, and use that to do what you need to presently. You've achieved before, you can again!

Respond: List past accomplishments.

Day 34

Accept ● Forward ● Practice ●

Inspire: Dream Everyday!

No matter what day of the week today is, pursue your dreams with a fire and passion you have on your favorite day! Dreams don't expire or take days off!

Respond: What can you dream today?

Day 35

Accept ● Forward ● Practice ●

Inspire: Alive to Live!

If you're reading this, you're alive, and being alive you're called to live! Be encouraged, and in so, encourage another to live! That thing that wants to bring you down doesn't want you to live for anything but it, which isn't living at all.

Respond: What wants to discourage you?

Day 36

Accept ● **Forward** ● **Practice** ●

Inspire: Read and Learn...

What do you read/watch? Is it positive? Or do you spend more time with news, fantasy, or darker things? Take a day away from it and find lighter fare, and see how you feel at the end of the day.

Respond: What have you put off reading?

Day 37

Accept ⬤ Forward ⬤ Practice ⬤

Inspire: The Impossible...

The only time you should use the word "impossible" is when saying, "It's *impossible* to stop me from achieving my dreams!" Make every dream possible, by knowing yourself and your true abilities.

Respond: List some possible dreams.

Day 38

Accept ● Forward ● Practice ●

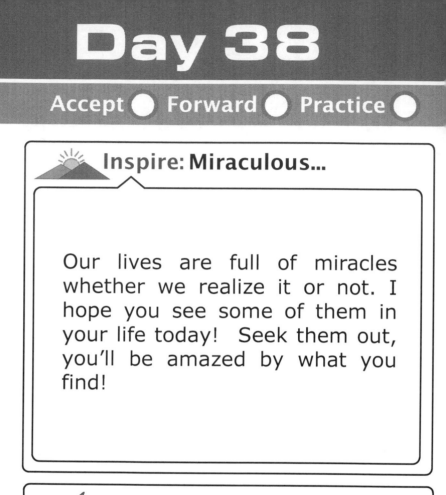

Inspire: Miraculous...

Our lives are full of miracles whether we realize it or not. I hope you see some of them in your life today! Seek them out, you'll be amazed by what you find!

Respond: What miracles have you seen?

Day 39

Inspire: Self Worth...

Don't question your worth in life, just know that you are of vital importance to those around you and many you've still not yet met. Feel the weight of your life today.

Respond: What impact have you made?

Day 40

Accept ● Forward ● Practice ●

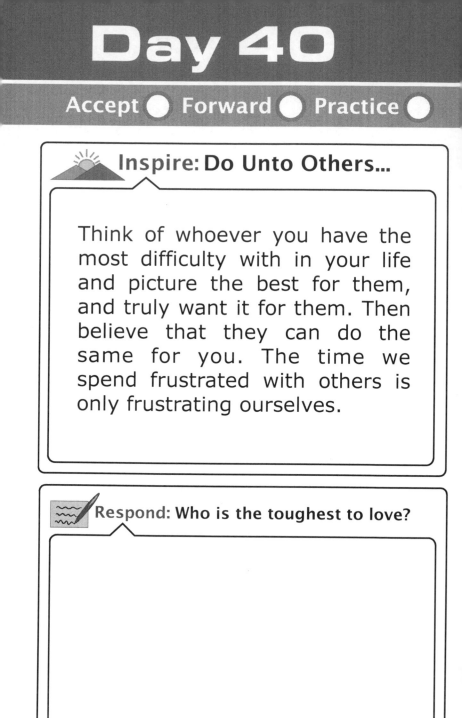

Inspire: Do Unto Others...

Think of whoever you have the most difficulty with in your life and picture the best for them, and truly want it for them. Then believe that they can do the same for you. The time we spend frustrated with others is only frustrating ourselves.

Respond: Who is the toughest to love?

Day 41

Inspire: Meant to Be...

Say this out loud, and believe it: "I was meant to be, and meant to do..." No matter how you came to be, you are here for a reason.

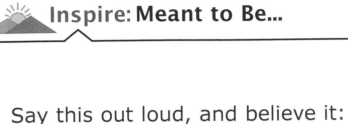

Respond: When do you feel important?

Day 42

Inspire: Purity...

A pure pursuit is the best way to achieve the truest goal. Remain true to what is right, good and just for everyone, not just yourself, and watch your growth!

Respond: What's pure about your goals?

Day 43

Inspire: Unburden Yourself...

Lay your burdens down before laying your head down. Give them up and awaken the next day free of the things that make you want to stay in bed.

Respond: What is a burden today?

Day 44

Inspire: Change...

Whatever you do today, do it with a belief that you can change the world for the better. And in so doing, change your world instantly!

Respond: What do you need to do today?

Day 45

Inspire: Healing Hurts...

When you are sad, know that all things in life have their moments, even those that make our hearts ache. Hurts can heal us from so much. Allow the full process of your hurts.

Respond: What is your biggest hurt?

Day 46

Inspire: Time to Listen...

Take some time and get as quiet as you can and listen to that still small voice. It may tell you something about yourself that you don't know.

Respond: What are you hearing inside?

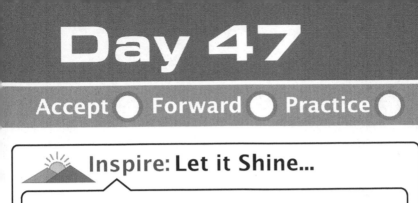

Day 47

Inspire: Let it Shine...

Wherever you are today and whatever you're doing, shine brightly and those around you won't be able to help but notice! And you will feel all the benefits!

Respond: How can you shine today?

Day 48

Accept ● Forward ● Practice ●

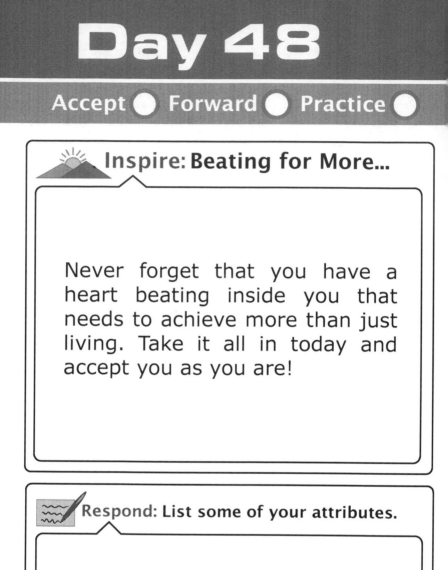

Inspire: Beating for More...

Never forget that you have a heart beating inside you that needs to achieve more than just living. Take it all in today and accept you as you are!

Respond: List some of your attributes.

Day 49

Inspire: What's Inside...

A new day. A new chance to put aside all the negative thoughts that come in and replace them with the positive, joyful thoughts that are hanging out inside you waiting for their cue!

Respond: What is hiding in you?

Day 50

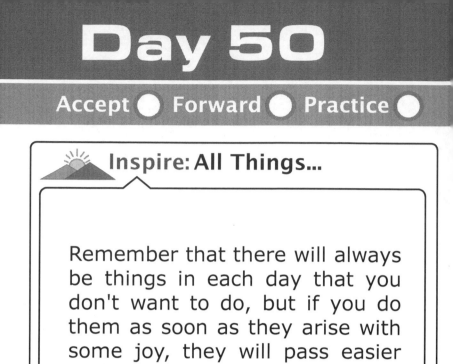

Inspire: All Things...

Remember that there will always be things in each day that you don't want to do, but if you do them as soon as they arise with some joy, they will pass easier and leave you relieved.

Respond: What don't you want to do?

Day 51

Inspire: Dream, Believe...

Dreams can be made into realities, so dream big and live even bigger! And believe.

Respond: What's your dream today?

Day 52

Accept ● Forward ● Practice ●

Inspire: Generational Hurts...

Know that family hurts don't have to be passed down. You can change the world that you live in and find escape from past experiences. Strive to find release and relief from negatives that surround your family tree.

Respond: What have you been holding?

Day 53

Accept ● Forward ● Practice ●

 Inspire: The Best of You...

Seek out the best, and the best will become your "normal", which will raise you to new levels and to succeed where you never thought possible!

 Respond: What is the best for you?

Day 54

Accept ● Forward ● Practice ●

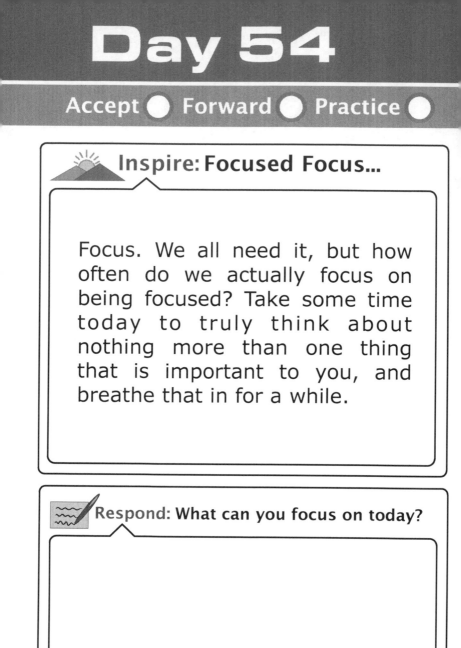

Inspire: Focused Focus...

Focus. We all need it, but how often do we actually focus on being focused? Take some time today to truly think about nothing more than one thing that is important to you, and breathe that in for a while.

Respond: What can you focus on today?

Day 55

Accept ● Forward ● Practice ●

Inspire: Never too Small...

I sometimes pray for a miracle that is big, and then I realize I'm missing all the little miracles that happen moment by moment throughout my day. See the big and small gifts you've been given today.

Respond: List some small "miracles".

Day 56

Accept ● Forward ● Practice ●

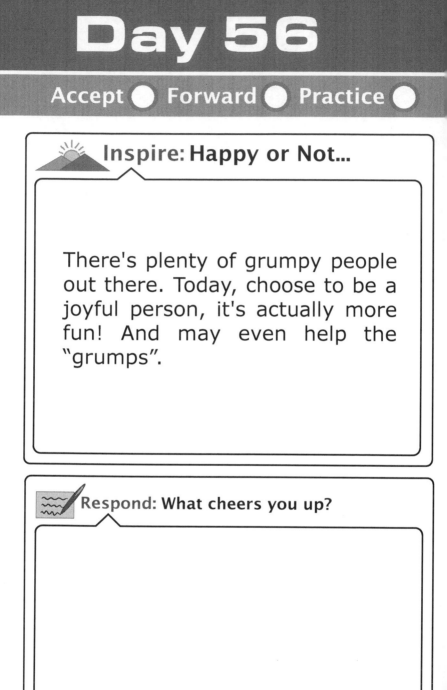

Inspire: Happy or Not...

There's plenty of grumpy people out there. Today, choose to be a joyful person, it's actually more fun! And may even help the "grumps".

Respond: What cheers you up?

Day 57

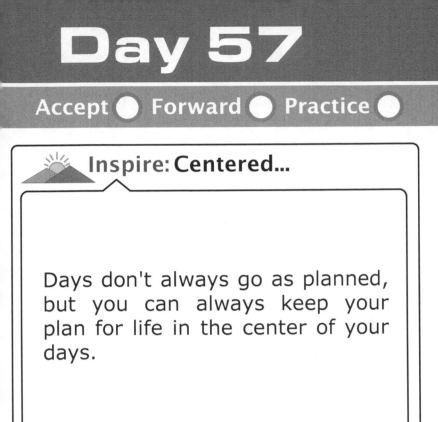

Inspire: Centered...

Days don't always go as planned, but you can always keep your plan for life in the center of your days.

Respond: What's your life plan?

Day 58

Inspire: Self Help...

The "self" may be the most elusive part of us. Find it in you and you will find who you are meant to be.

Respond: Who do you see you as?

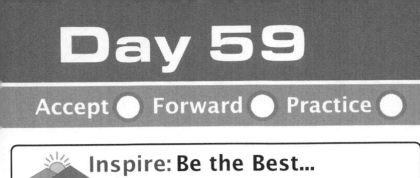

Day 59

Accept ● Forward ● Practice ●

Inspire: Be the Best...

By all means that are good, noble and true, be your dream. Accomplish what lays in front of you today so others can accomplish even more tomorrow.

Respond: What can you pass down?

Day 60

Accept ● Forward ● Practice ●

☀ Inspire: Let Me Believe...

If you can't believe in yourself today, know that I believe in you. You took the time to read my book, I'll take the time to pray for your best! You CAN DO IT!! Never give up!

✎ Respond: Breathe in that others love you.

Day 61

Inspire: Another Day...

When it feels like "just another day" remember it's actually another opportunity to try new things and to enjoy the old things.

Respond: List old accomplishments.

Day 62

Accept ● Forward ● Practice ●

 Inspire: Imagine & Live...

I believe, our imagination is a God given gift. Don't let yours stray from the goals of achieving greatness in your reality!

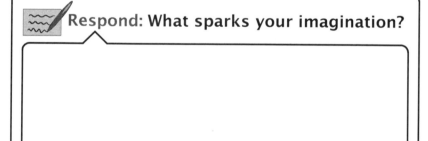 Respond: What sparks your imagination?

Day 63

Accept ● Forward ● Practice ●

 Inspire: Name Your Best...

What are the best things you have going for you right now? Write them down and see the blessings in front of you today!

Respond: What "best" is in front of you?

Accept ● Forward ● Practice ●

 **Inspire: Daily Dreams...**

Know your dreams and pursue them with the same energy and force as your daily tasks. Make them a normal part of your thoughts and goals, and they will become a reality.

Respond: List some dreams to pursue.

Day 65

Accept ● Forward ● Practice ●

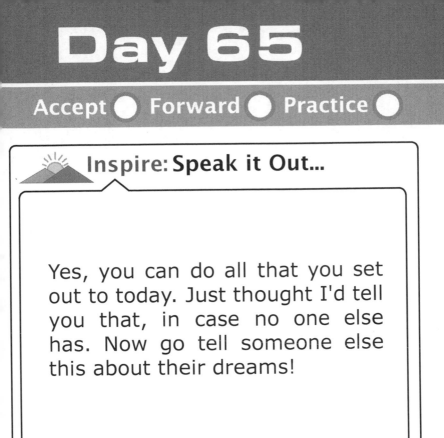

Inspire: Speak it Out...

Yes, you can do all that you set out to today. Just thought I'd tell you that, in case no one else has. Now go tell someone else this about their dreams!

Respond: Who can you encourage today?

Day 66

Accept ● Forward ● Practice ●

Inspire: Delightful Detours...

There will be detours today in your plans. Know that, and treat them as mini adventures instead of major annoyances.

Respond: How can you stay positive?

Day 67

Accept ● Forward ● Practice ●

Inspire: Inch by Inch...

If you cannot fulfill or complete your *big* dream today, ask yourself what you can do to at least start or begin to chip away at it.

Respond: What small step can you make?

Day 68

Inspire: With Feeling!

Today is the perfect day for you to achieve something you've never done before. Anything! Memorize a positive thought, tackle a project at home you've put off, step out and tell someone they're awesome, or simply go to a quiet place outside, away from others and feel the wind, sun, rain, whatever the weather is and let it sink into you. Feel LIFE!

Respond: What will it be?

Day 69

Accept ● Forward ● Practice ●

Inspire: A Logical Dream...

If you are hungry... you eat. If you are cold... you put on a jacket. If you are sleepy... you go to bed, etc., etc. So if you have a dream... why not pursue it with the same simple logic. It's the only way to make it happen. Go after it!

Respond: How will you pursue <u>you</u> today?

Day 70

Accept ● Forward ● Practice ●

Inspire: Who's Next?

Who are you today? What makes up your identity? Know the answer to that question. Knowing what you are truly about will help you accomplish your true goals. If you see that you are more of what you don't want to be, then write those traits down and see how you can rid yourself of them daily. Again, if you believe the best you will draw the best to you!

 Respond: List your best traits.

Day 71

Inspire: Let it Be...

Life can be awesome! Just don't hold so tight to all that you think it should be, and just let it be.

Respond: What do you need to let go of?

Day 72

 Inspire: Time for Time...

Take some time today, to do exactly that... enjoy the *time* given you. Life is a gift and it can be beautiful, if we take the time to see it that way.

 Respond: What has time brought you?

Day 73

Inspire: Fear Not...

Walk today without fear and see how much farther in your journey you get. Fear is not a necessity, it is a by-product of disbelief. Believe.

Respond: What are you fearing today?

Day 74

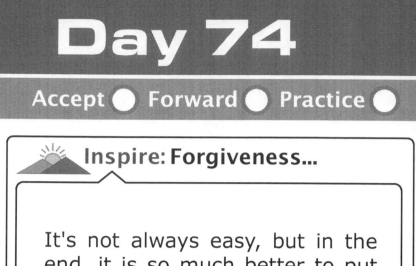

Inspire: Forgiveness...

It's not always easy, but in the end, it is so much better to put aside anger and remember we all fall short of the glory. If you haven't, do your best to forgive someone this week; it hurts you more than them to not.

Respond: Who can you forgive today?

Day 75

Accept ● Forward ● Practice ●

Inspire: Right to do Right...

When you're not sure if something is right to do, ask yourself who it benefits most and why. If you can see it being for the greater good, then go for it. Just make sure the good is greater for more than you alone.

Respond: Who else will your good help?

Day 76

 Inspire: Believing in More...

Believe in yourself. But believe that what you're really striving for is to do more for others than for yourself. In so doing, you will see a reason to believe.

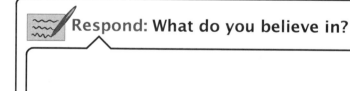 Respond: What do you believe in?

Day 77

Inspire: Simple Beliefs...

Take time to focus in on what you hope to accomplish this week, then simply believe that you will accomplish it. A positive outlook on the challenges of day-to-day life and a belief in doing, is going to get you to your end goal. I believe you can do it!

Respond: Where's your focus today?

Day 78

Accept ● Forward ● Practice ●

Inspire: A Thought for You...

There are plenty of people that will never do what they truly desire, but there are not enough people that do what can change the world. You can. Know that there are people you've never met that will one day be affected by you, and what you've accomplished... if you do it.

 Respond: Who has affected your life?

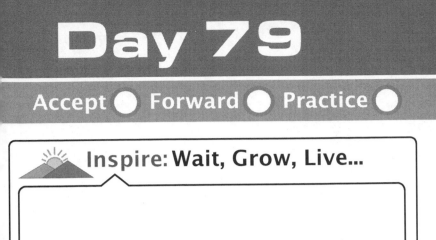

Inspire: Wait, Grow, Live...

If you're waiting for something today, know that in the waiting is where we grow, so embrace the wait, and find peace with what you're learning through the process.

Respond: What has kept you waiting?

Day 80

Accept ● Forward ● Practice ●

Inspire: This is the Time...

We can never become all we strive to be if we constantly look at it as unachievable in the present. Believe you can do it now and start today! Before you know it, "now" will be when you did it!

Respond: List what you want now.

Day 81

Accept ● Forward ● Practice ●

Inspire: Mirror, Mirror...

Even if you don't want to... go to a mirror and smile at yourself. Goofy? Maybe a little, but it will change your outlook... Your smile is what shows others your joy. See what they see when you're happy.

Respond: How do you see you?

Day 82

Inspire: Why Worry?

If I say to you, "Don't worry about..." Will you do it anyway? And what will the "..." be? Remember, no one ever takes their last breath thinking, "I wish I worried more in life".

Respond: What's the "..." in your worry?

Day 83

Accept ● Forward ● Practice ●

Inspire: On Again, Off Again...

Use the things that excite you in life to get something done that you've put off, today. Putting things off can take more energy than doing them, because it creates more stress and stress is an energy killer.

Respond: How do you react to stress?

Day 84

Accept ● Forward ● Practice ●

Inspire: Get What You Give...

Give something to someone today that is truly from your heart, and see what happens. Chances are you'll be given something of the same or even greater value back.

Respond: What can you give? And to who?

Inspire: Stop the Words...

See if you can go thru today without saying things like, "I hate..." or "I'm bad at..." Anything that's negative towards you or others, fast from it. We actually say things "off the cuff" more than we think. Give it a shot and see how you feel tonight. Good luck!

Respond: Replace negative words with...?

Day 86

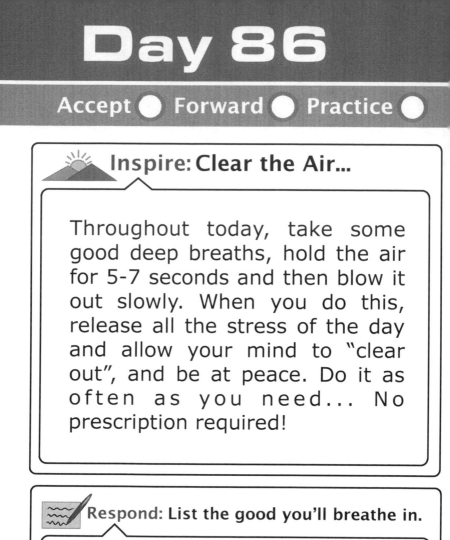

Inspire: Clear the Air...

Throughout today, take some good deep breaths, hold the air for 5-7 seconds and then blow it out slowly. When you do this, release all the stress of the day and allow your mind to "clear out", and be at peace. Do it as often as you need... No prescription required!

Respond: List the good you'll breathe in.

Day 87

 **Inspire: Clean House...**

Get rid of all that creates negativity in you! You can accomplish that next big hurdle in your life, it's waiting on the other side of the burdens we create.

Respond: List the top things to get rid of.

Day 88

Accept ● Forward ● Practice ●

Inspire: Easy vs. Hard...

What stretches you more in life? The hard stuff? Or the easy? Endure the tough stuff, it will make you stronger on the other side, and the easy will seem even easier!

Respond: What's the hardest stuff today?

Day 89

Accept ● Forward ● Practice ●

Inspire: One at a Time...

So many things to do today, but rather than over-thinking all of them, pick one that can be finished before doing anything else, and finish it. And then use it to build confidence for the rest. Don't let life get in the way of living.

Respond: First task today to finish is?

Day 90

Accept ● Forward ● Practice ●

Inspire: One Step Closer...

Stop, look around you and ask, "Have I accomplished what I've set out to this week?" If not, look to each moment as a new chance to begin a new portion of the bigger picture, and relax, it will get done with this attitude. You can do it, and it will be great!

Respond: List new ways to get it done.

Day 91

Accept ● Forward ● Practice ●

Inspire: Give, Receive...

Who can you encourage right now? You? A friend? Perhaps a stranger? Take this moment either via text, e-mail, phone or in person to encourage someone else! We get what we give; give encouragement!

Respond: Who did you encourage? How?

Day 92

Accept ● Forward ● Practice ●

Inspire: Ready to Achieve...

How do you see you? Someone that is waiting for someone else to bring you that "perfect opportunity" or someone that is looking to make that moment themselves? No one can be you and no one can make things your way. Be you and be alive and ready for more than waiting. Go for it!

Respond: What's your perfect moment?

Day 93

Inspire: We Live, We Learn...

I don't always have the answers to life, but that's how I know I'm learning, through the trials that my missteps bring me. Embrace the trials as much as the peace and you will find what you've learned and acquire more peace.

Respond: What mistake became a plus?

Day 94

 **Inspire: In a Moment...**

After you read this, take a moment to get by yourself and be quiet, breathe, relax, and give thanks. Then refocus whatever you were going to do with that peace in mind.

Respond: What are you thankful for?

Day 95

Accept ● Forward ● Practice ○

Inspire: Read and Achieve...

If you haven't done it today, acknowledge the fact that you have achieved something, even if that "something" is simply reading this. You can use this positive thought pattern to develop the muscle within you to see positives over negatives, and in turn, accomplish even more!

Respond: List some positive words.

Day 96

Accept ● Forward ● Practice ●

 Inspire: Next is Now...

Today, focus on... Today. We can spend so much time thinking about what's next, or what happened in the past, we miss what's right in front of us. I see a day full of potential to accomplish another task! Hope you see the same.

Respond: What's in front of you today?

Day 97

 **Inspire: Big Patience...**

What do you do when you're waiting? Do you get impatient? Or do you look to the wait as something that builds your endurance and strength in the day-to-day of life? Be patient for the big stuff and enjoy the little things along the way!

Respond: What's your next big thing?

Day 98

Accept ● Forward ● Practice ○

☀ Inspire: No Matter What...

Whatever the weather, your condition, financial, marital, dating, or working status; you have the option to stay positive. In doing so, you may also encourage someone else that doesn't see that option today. Happiness can be accomplished and spread to others by acknowledging the good. It's out there, see it!

 Respond: What makes you rejoice?

Day 99

Accept ● Forward ● Practice ●

Inspire: It's All a Part of It...

You can achieve the best possible outcome in every situation today! Just remember that everything you do, right and wrong, are part of the learning experience and while you shouldn't excuse the wrong, use it to make you wiser. Learn from all that you do today and write down what worked and what didn't. Then read as needed.

Respond: What did and didn't work today?

Day 100

Accept ● Forward ● Practice ●

Inspire: Keep Going!

100 days! You've stuck with it this long, keep going and see how a daily dose of positivity can encourage, enlighten, and expand your dreams and goals, even further; as well as make them even more possible! Thank you for sticking with it!

Respond: What have you achieved so far?

Day 101

Accept ● Forward ● Practice ●

Inspire: Time Will Remain...

If it's hard to do today, it doesn't mean it's impossible to do tomorrow. Patience and wisdom can be yours, use every moment of life to learn.

Respond: List attributes of patience.

Day 102

Inspire: Leap Over It...

Sometimes the things we're fearing most are actually the smallest hurdles, when put into perspective. Write down a hurdle and see how small it really is when it's just a word or two on paper. Then crumple it up and throw it away, figuratively and literally.

Respond: How did it feel to throw it away?

Day 103

Accept ● Forward ● Practice ●

Inspire: Love and Live...

The world needs you today. Give it what you can and remember that even those that have annoyed you have someone that annoys them, and you both have those that love you. Some may love you both. It's easy to be annoyed, it's stronger to love no matter what! Grab this life and shake it up!

Respond: Who can make you stronger?

Day 104

Accept ● Forward ● Practice ●

Inspire: This is Your Day...

I have an amazing day ahead of me and so do you! How do I know? Well, we're alive and any day you're alive can be amazing! Believe that it can be!

Respond: What's amazing about today?

Day 105

 **Inspire: Question Yourself...**

Ask yourself daily, "What is my motivation for doing what I'm doing?" Then, find things to do that fit into the answer, "To make life better for more than just me."

Respond: What will make life better?

Day 106

Accept ● Forward ● Practice ●

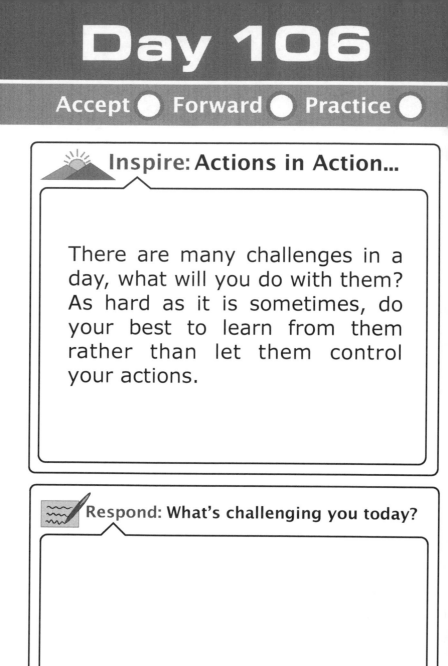

Inspire: Actions in Action...

There are many challenges in a day, what will you do with them? As hard as it is sometimes, do your best to learn from them rather than let them control your actions.

Respond: What's challenging you today?

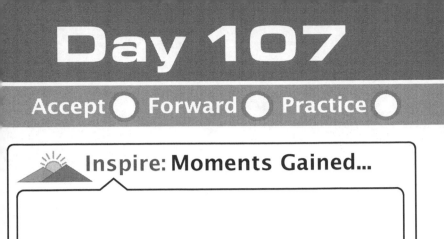

Day 107

Accept ● Forward ● Practice ●

Inspire: **Moments Gained...**

Take a moment today to simply stop and feel life around you. It is in those moments that we can tune into what we really should be doing, and how to go about it.

Respond: What did you gain by stopping?

Day 108

Accept ● Forward ● Practice ●

Inspire: Do the Hard Stuff...

What's the toughest thing you could do right now that would help you do more with your life? What are you going to do to go after it? Don't miss these parts of life, they do mean something.

.

Respond: What is the toughest thing?

Day 109

Accept ● Forward ● Practice ●

Inspire: Spread it Around...

Remember you can't control how others think, act, or live. But you can control how *you* do. Live joyfully today, it may just rub off on someone else!

Respond: What's controlling you today?

Day 110

Accept ● Forward ● Practice ●

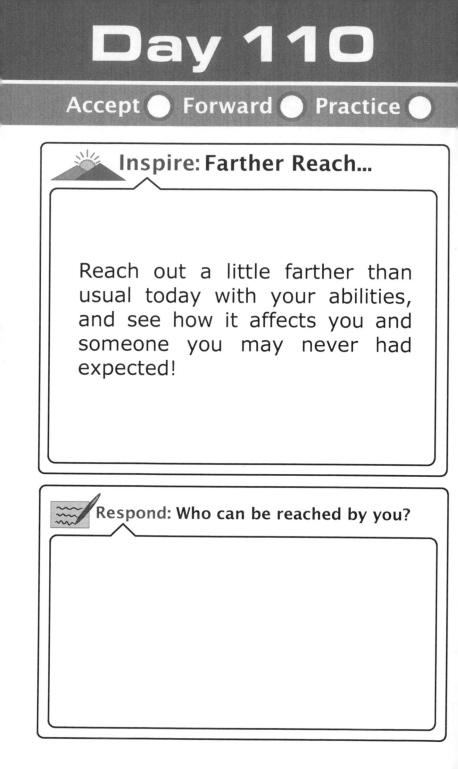

Inspire: Farther Reach...

Reach out a little farther than usual today with your abilities, and see how it affects you and someone you may never had expected!

Respond: Who can be reached by you?

Day 111

Accept ● Forward ● Practice ●

Inspire: It All Counts...

Every one of us matters. Every one of us counts. Believe it for yourself, but also for all those that you encounter today. If you can, believe in them, and know that someone else is believing in you too.

Respond: List some people to believe in.

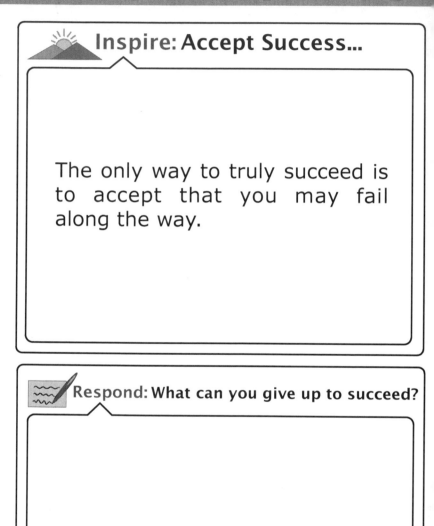

Inspire: Accept Success...

The only way to truly succeed is to accept that you may fail along the way.

Respond: What can you give up to succeed?

Day 113

Accept ● Forward ● Practice ●

Inspire: Who's Doing?

What do you see in this life that makes you angry, or ask "why?" What of your time and energy can you apply to these things to stop them from just being frustrations and become accomplishments. If not you then who?

Respond: What can you change right now?

Day 114

Accept ● Forward ● Practice ●

Inspire: At the Day's End...

The end of a busy day can be the beginning of a peaceful night. Tonight, confidently enter your evening knowing you did good, and it's okay to rest. Anxious thoughts of the day will not bring a restful night.

Respond: What was accomplished today?

Day 115

Accept ● Forward ● Practice ●

Inspire: Hurts and Healing...

Seek the truth in your life no matter what! Even if it means looking at things you want to avoid, it will always bring true healing! It hurts for a reason, it needs to be fixed, and then healed.

Respond: What needs fixing?

Day 116

Inspire: Build Bigger...

Say out loud at least 5 times today, "I can and will accomplish all that I have set in front of me today." Then believe it, and make sure what you have set in front of you is achievable, as to not create failure. You can be the person you set out to be, through simple daily achievements that build to a bigger goal.

 Respond: What other positives can you say?

Day 117

Inspire: No Mistakes...

No matter what anyone says, you are not a mistake, nor are your dreams and goals. Tell yourself that today... and believe.

Respond: List your goals and dreams.

Day 118

Inspire: Everything Counts...

As many times as you've made a mistake, you've also learned and grown. There's nothing wrong with stumbling if you can use it for future success and growth.

Respond: What are you learning?

Day 119

Accept ● Forward ● Practice ●

Inspire: Clarity in the Noise...

Clouded thoughts are to be expected when you're looking for clarity. Know that you're on the right track when you can't get it right the first time, but are trying. Truth and clear thinking will win the day if you believe in it!

Respond: What is becoming clearer?

Day 120

Accept ● Forward ● Practice ●

Inspire: Listen and Learn...

It's hard to hear criticism, but it's harder to live without a true picture of one's self. Let truth rule no matter how it feels at first.

Respond: What critique has helped you?

 **Inspire: Say it, Repeat it...**

"Today I will do my best to stay away from the negative and positively seek truth, vision, forgiveness, and belief in my dreams and goals."

Respond: Write another positive statement.

Day 122

Accept ● Forward ● Practice ●

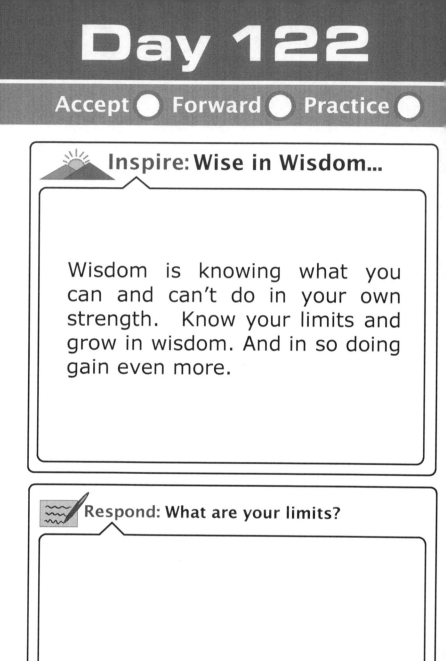

Inspire: Wise in Wisdom...

Wisdom is knowing what you can and can't do in your own strength. Know your limits and grow in wisdom. And in so doing gain even more.

Respond: What are your limits?

Day 123

Accept ● Forward ● Practice ●

Inspire: Talking to Yourself...

How do you look at yourself? What do you see? Take a long look today and tell yourself that you are confident, strong, decisive, and kind. Then, remember this conversation and those words will find you when you need them.

Respond: Are there more words to add?

Day 124

Accept ● Forward ● Practice ●

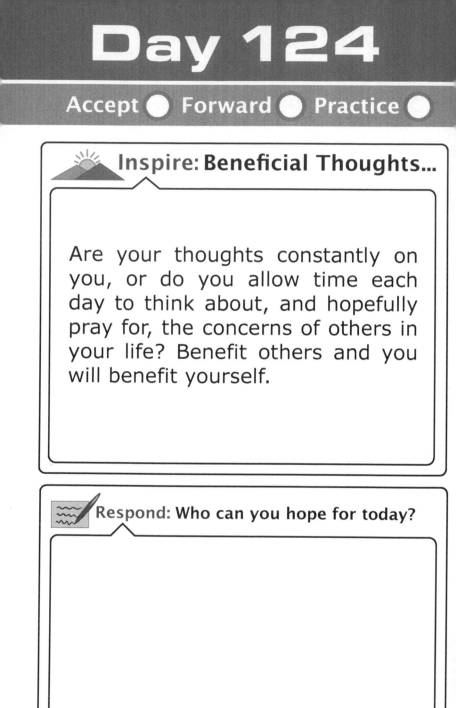

Inspire: Beneficial Thoughts...

Are your thoughts constantly on you, or do you allow time each day to think about, and hopefully pray for, the concerns of others in your life? Benefit others and you will benefit yourself.

Respond: Who can you hope for today?

Day 125

Accept ● Forward ● Practice ●

Inspire: **Believe.**

We can feel so many things in even a moment, but can we learn to simply feel one thing... True happiness? Reach for it and let go of all the other thoughts that crowd your mind from moment to moment. You can do it!

Respond: **What does happiness look like?**

Day 126

Accept ● Forward ● Practice ●

Inspire: The Call...

We're not always aware of the call on our lives until someone else is in need. In the light of this day find what moves you and embrace it. Seek your calling.

Respond: What is your calling?

Day 127

Accept ● Forward ● Practice ●

Inspire: Your New Name...

What words come to mind when you think of you? When you fill your thoughts with forgiveness, joy, hope, and truth, you will hopefully call yourself by a new name: "Healed".

Respond: Words that encourage you are?

Day 128

Accept ● Forward ● Practice ●

Inspire: Say It...

What have you always wanted to say that you can't get yourself to speak? Say it now, while you're alone, speak it out and if it's good, let it penetrate you. If it's bad... Be done with it, and do your best to never say it again.

Respond: How did you feel speaking it out?

Day 129

Inspire: Imitation for Real...

If you just can't believe the best for yourself, imitate the belief and it's actions, and before you know it, you may just stop pretending and start believing.

Respond: What would you like to be?

Day 130

Inspire: Mercy Me...

Mercy is something we all want and cry out for when we're really at the bottom. Are you offering mercy to someone today that in your opinion doesn't deserve it? Try it and see who they become.

Respond: Write words of mercy for them.

Day 131

Accept ● Forward ● Practice ●

Inspire: More than Money...

Instead of wanting more of life's material things, want, seek, breathe in the things that cost nothing... Beauty, grace, joy, happiness, truth, wisdom, knowledge, understanding, forgiveness... Love. Once you've acquired these things, give them out to everyone for free!

Respond: What are your free gifts?

Day 132

Accept ● Forward ● Practice ●

Inspire: Turn Back Time...

You can't go back and become more of what you wanted to be, but you can repair it with forgiveness... of not just others, but yourself. Today, let yourself forgive you and see time move forward.

Respond: What do you need to forgive?

Day 133

Inspire: Your Time, Now...

There is a moment that you can hold onto and live in... It's right now! It changes with every second! Take it and enjoy it! Don't think about yesterday's troubles or tomorrow's what ifs. Simply live in this time with the belief that you are alive and well for a reason.

Respond: What's happening right now?

Day 134

Accept ● Forward ● Practice ●

Inspire: Time to Find Time...

"Time off" gives us time to get away from all the "things" we *feel* we "must" do... But remember, pure and simple rest is a must too! Find the time this week to rest your soul from life's frantic pace.

Respond: What do you need to rest from?

Day 135

Inspire: Your Choice...

Today can be amazing! So take it in and let all the things you don't want out. Remember we can choose to be happy no matter what. It's not always easy, but it is possible. Be blessed!

Respond: What's amazing about today?

Day 136

 **Inspire: Challenge Accepted!**

When life gives you a difficulty, grab it and search it for the best parts and believe that's why you have been given the challenge. To grow from it and endure it with patience. You can do it!

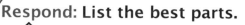 **Respond: List the best parts.**

Day 137

Accept ● Forward ● Practice ●

Inspire: Live Out Loud!

Say every hour today, "I am alive to accomplish more than just living! I am grateful for life! I will live my life 'out loud'! I *will* accomplish more!" And believe it when you say it!

Respond: How does it feel to live?

Day 138

Accept ● Forward ● Practice ●

Inspire: Positive People...

There will always be negative people, with negative thoughts about you, others, and even themselves. You don't have to be one of them or be around them. Find the positive people in your life and stick to them.

Respond: Who will you seek out?

Day 139

Accept ● Forward ● Practice ●

Inspire: Best of the Least...

What is your favorite part of the day? What does it make you feel and why? Now take all this information and apply it to your least favorite parts. Believe they will change, and then start changing them.

Respond: Best parts of the best parts are?

Day 140

Accept ● Forward ● Practice ●

Inspire: Make History...

Make today a red letter date in your history by changing at least one negative to a positive for the long term. Do this by not allowing the negative thoughts about it to become stuck in your mind. When it comes up, fight it with a positive word or action. And again... Believe.

Respond: List the positives you'll use.

Day 141

Accept ● Forward ● Practice ●

Inspire: The Day Before...

Make this the day after you changed for good to be good, truthful, and happy. And now that it's here... LIVE IT!!

Respond: List the negatives you gave up.

Day 142

Accept ● Forward ● Practice ●

 **Inspire: Not the End...**

The end of relationships, jobs, stories, is also the beginning of new adventures. Take what you've learned from the ones ending and use the knowledge in your new endeavors.

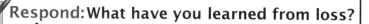 **Respond: What have you learned from loss?**

Day 143

Accept ● Forward ● Practice ●

Inspire: By Your Side...

Who is by you through all your life's troubles, adventures, trials, joys, and pains? Take a moment today and write them a quick note to remind them how much they mean to you. Love is the most powerful thing we can possess.

Respond: What do you want to tell them?

Day 144

Accept ● Forward ● Practice ●

Inspire: Rest not Ragged...

Do you conflict with yourself to stay motivated, but to also find the time to relax? Remember the way to true accomplishment is with health and refreshment to the body. Take time to rest your body and mind. We can run till we're ragged, or rest and run another day. Oh, and wash your hands a lot too! :)

Respond: What can you set aside today?

Day 145

Accept ● Forward ● Practice ●

Inspire: Dig Down Deep...

Sometimes the challenge in your life may be finding what challenges you. Pursue a deeper dream today!

Respond: What would be a new challenge?

Day 146

Accept ● Forward ● Practice ●

Inspire: Leave it Behind You...

What can you pack up and leave behind today? Anger? Pain? Grief? Loss? Unforgiven wounds? Take the time to fully visual your life without these things... How would that be?

Respond: What new dreams can you begin?

Day 147

Accept ● Forward ● Practice ●

Inspire: The Other Foot...

Remember today that you never know what that person that's rubbing you the wrong way is going through on their end. If you can take the time you'd spend thinking about them in the negative and change it to the positive, you may just see a change in both of you.

 Respond: Write some positives about them.

Day 148

Accept ● Forward ● Practice ●

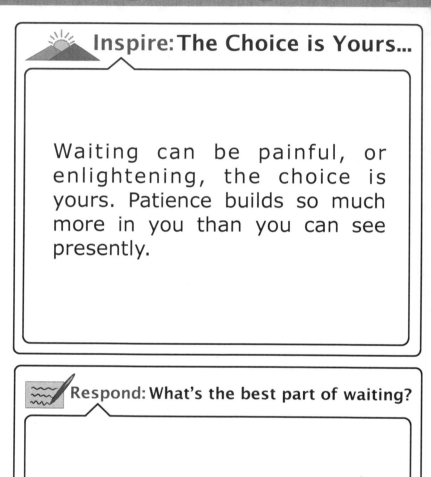

Inspire: The Choice is Yours...

Waiting can be painful, or enlightening, the choice is yours. Patience builds so much more in you than you can see presently.

Respond: What's the best part of waiting?

Day 149

Accept ● Forward ● Practice ●

Inspire: It's Here Now!

No matter what difficulty you're going through presently, know that there is also something positive going on in your life right now. Find out what it is and take some time to think about it, and be grateful!

Respond: Where are your positives?

Day 150

Accept ● Forward ● Practice ●

**Inspire: Your Plan, Right Now!**

Whatever you're planning right now, plan it with the goal to succeed! Your first success today was getting to the 150th day of this book! Keep going!

**Respond: What is your plan right now?**

Day 151

Accept ● Forward ● Practice ●

Inspire: Anxiety Be Gone...

"Anxiety." Even saying it brings it up. A very wise man once said not to be anxious... and He meant it. The reason being, it adds nothing to our life... except "anxiety". If you have anxiety, breathe, and tell yourself, this will pass... Trust me, it will.

Respond: What are you anxious about?

Day 152

Accept ● Forward ● Practice ●

Inspire: Do What You Love...

It should never be hard to do what you love, but getting the chances to do it can be. Keep at it and never give up!

Respond: What's your favorite thing?

Day 153

Accept ● Forward ● Practice ●

 **Inspire: Help Me, Help You...**

It's not always easy to motivate yourself, so make sure you have plenty of others to help you! And in turn help them with what they love! When you help others you shine a little brighter!

Respond: Where can you help someone?

Day 154

 **Inspire:Pleasantly Unpleasant...**

Many things that seem unpleasant are really to help us in the long term. What difficult or painful thing do you have to deal with today that will truly make you stronger and better off?

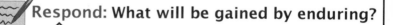 **Respond: What will be gained by enduring?**

Day 155

Accept ● Forward ● Practice ●

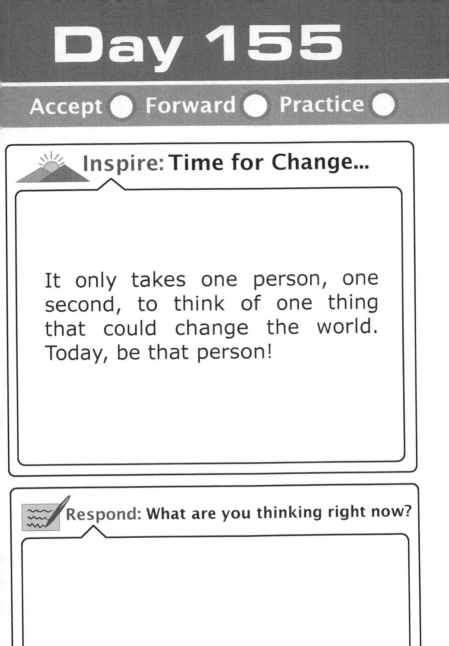

Inspire: Time for Change...

It only takes one person, one second, to think of one thing that could change the world. Today, be that person!

Respond: What are you thinking right now?

Day 156

Accept ● Forward ● Practice ●

Inspire: I Believe...

Tell the voice that says, "can't" to, "leave". There are people believing in you right at this moment. Believe in you too!

Respond: What needs to leave your mind?

Day 157

Accept ● Forward ● Practice ●

Inspire: Wake Up!!

Find and do the things that invigorate you! Sing in the shower, or car... Go for a ride or walk. Run, dance, jump... Be a goof! And most importantly... Laugh with someone today!

Respond: Make a list of fun things to do.

Day 158

Accept ● Forward ● Practice ●

Inspire: Barefoot in the Park...

Take a moment today to take off your shoes and feel the earth on your feet. Sounds strange? Perhaps, but connecting this way can help center you when you're stuck being... stuck.

Respond: Where's your favorite place?

Day 159

Accept ● Forward ● Practice ●

Inspire: The Thick of It...

When you're in the middle of a stressful or unpleasant moment in your life, take time to be thankful that it will not last forever. All this too will pass, and the greater will emerge.

Respond: What negatives will pass?

Day 160

Inspire: Past to Present...

Think of *(or better yet, write down)* all the reasons doing what you've been putting off could help you and others. Then use that to move forward with the belief that you can accomplish even a portion of it this week! You can, look at all you've done in the past and use it to motivate your future!

Respond: Write it here!

Day 161

Accept ● Forward ● Practice ●

Inspire: Create a Challenge...

If we didn't have challenges, where would we be? Challenges create possibilities in us! Think about it for a minute and then think about what benefit your challenges are bringing you today! Embrace them, they make you stronger!

Respond: List some challenges.

Day 162

Accept ● Forward ● Practice ●

Inspire: Best Day to Do It...

Today is a good day to believe in all that you aspire to. Take even a few minutes today to affirm in yourself that you can achieve all that you are going after, and that it's for the betterment of the world around you! You can do it!

Respond: What do you aspire to?

Day 163

Accept ● Forward ● Practice ●

Inspire: Believe it or Not...

We have a choice each day to believe a better way is either around the corner, straight ahead, or already here. But we also can believe it will never come... They're all choices, but not all should be chosen. Choose the most positive, and feel it live in you!

Respond: Where is your choice today?

Day 164

Accept ● Forward ● Practice ●

Inspire: What's Your Story?

Take some time to look at the "story of your life" so far and see what plot points you'd like to add, subtract, re-write, or even re-publish. It's your story, but remember it's also your legacy. Make it truthful and redemptive to all the characters.

Respond: Where is your story taking you?

Day 165

Accept ● Forward ● Practice ●

Inspire: Words of Life...

If you have the breath in you to speak out a negative, you also have it to speak out and live a positive. Choose positive and truly live!

Respond: List some positive words.

Day 166

Inspire: Emotion, Less...

There are times when it would seem the world would want us to give out less emotion, less reality, less soul. It is those times when the world needs you and your gifts all the more. To find who you are, be you, and practice it.

 Respond: How can you be more you?

Day 167

Accept ● Forward ● Practice ●

Inspire: Guilty of Guilt...

Are we so stuck on guilt that we can't see where forgiveness of ourselves comes in? Don't allow yourself to get stuck in guilt. Release your guilt by admitting to all your wrongs and seek forgiveness, not just from others but yourself.

Respond: What do you need to forgive?

Day 168

Accept ● Forward ● Practice ●

Inspire: Admit and Omit...

Life is not always going to be easy. How you handle it may not always be right. Remembering we're human, holding to honesty, being willing to be wrong, and admitting it when it happens, will always make life better in the long run.

Respond: What have you been wrong about?

Day 169

Accept ● Forward ● Practice ●

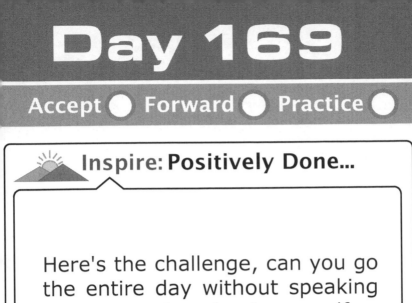

Inspire: Positively Done...

Here's the challenge, can you go the entire day without speaking out a negative about yourself or others? Truly try. If you don't make it, try again... Everyday. It's the effort that heals.

Respond: List some positives to think of.

Day 170

Inspire: Life in Reverse...

If you're trying to figure out what to do first today, make a list starting with what can be done last, and work backwards until you get to the most important part. Then give your full attention to it now that the other things have been written out as well.

Respond: What's the biggest goal today?

Day 171

Accept ● Forward ● Practice ●

Inspire: A New Day...

It's the perfect day to achieve something you have never achieved before! Even if that something is thinking in a positive way towards your goals!

Respond: What's your impossible, why?

Day 172

Accept ● Forward ● Practice ●

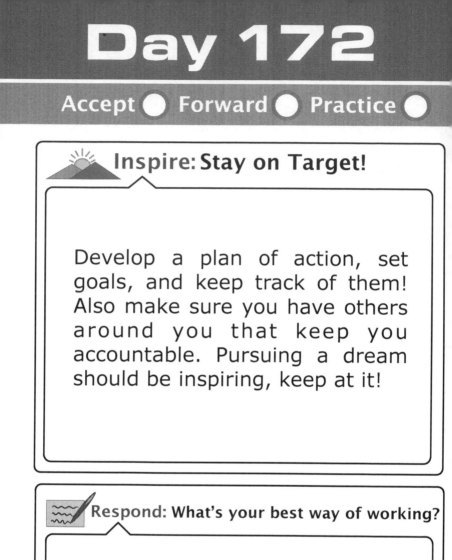

Inspire: Stay on Target!

Develop a plan of action, set goals, and keep track of them! Also make sure you have others around you that keep you accountable. Pursuing a dream should be inspiring, keep at it!

Respond: What's your best way of working?

Day 173

Accept ● Forward ● Practice ●

Inspire: Plain and Simply...

Even when you don't feel like it... Hold tight to the positives in life! I know I don't always want to either, but when I do I sure feel the difference! Hang in there, it will matter in the long run.

Respond: What's challenging you now?

Day 174

Accept ● Forward ● Practice ●

Inspire: One Down...

Today is another chance to be the person you're striving to be! Believe you can do more today, even if it's one thing you've put off for awhile, do your best to check it off the list!

Respond: Why should you believe today?

Day 175

Accept ● Forward ● Practice ●

Inspire: A Good Day For...

Some days are simply for trying to figure out who you are, who you want to be and where you want to go with your life. Today is as good a day as any for doing that! Make notes today, so you can see later where and how you've changed.

Respond: Who are you, what do you want?

Day 176

Accept ● Forward ● Practice ●

 Inspire: It's all a Part of It...

I know it's hard to be happy all the time, so remember sadness, anger, and frustrations are a part of life as well. When you feel them, understand them, and look to the goal of putting them aside when they have run their course. Then hold onto what brings you joy and let go of the negative. Let it go!

Respond: What changes your thoughts?

Day 177

Accept ● Forward ● Practice ●

Inspire: **Passion & Pursuit...**

Pursue everything with passion and that passion will pursue you. I am passionate about inspiring others, what are you passionate about?

Respond: **Your Passions...**

Day 178

Accept ● Forward ● Practice ○

Inspire: Listen & Hear...

Sometimes it's good to simply start the day with a favorite piece of music. Something that makes you feel inspired, happy. Hear what it's telling you and make notes about your feelings. I'm listening to some right now!

Respond: What are you hearing?

Day 179

Accept ● Forward ● Practice ●

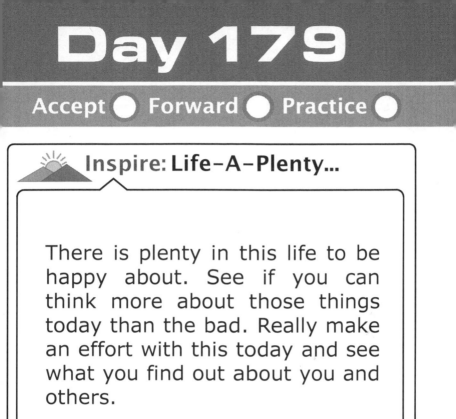

Inspire: Life–A–Plenty...

There is plenty in this life to be happy about. See if you can think more about those things today than the bad. Really make an effort with this today and see what you find out about you and others.

Respond: What are you happy about?

Day 180

Inspire: Think of it this Way...

It's a great day to start a new way of thinking if your old way has negative thoughts in it. May joy, peace, and kindness be in the forefront of your mind this day! Replace the negative with those words, watch the results and believe.

Respond: List more replacement words.

Day 181

Accept ● Forward ● Practice ●

Inspire: It All Matters...

Plan for your success, and count everything good and bad as experience towards your ultimate goal. It all matters and makes us better if we apply it towards our dreams!

Respond: What can you apply today?

Day 182

Accept ● Forward ● Practice ●

Inspire: It's Inside...

What is your goal for life and are you making daily adjustments to achieve it? If you don't know your goal, set out to find it! You can do it! It's in you; ask and you shall receive.

Respond: Goals & Dreams?

Day 183

Accept ● Forward ● Practice ●

Inspire: Stop, Look, Listen...

There's a great line in a movie that goes something like, "Are you someone that waits to talk or one who listens to what's being said?" One of them will help you achieve your dreams and goals.

Respond: When have you listened well?

Day 184

Accept ● Forward ● Practice ●

Inspire: Fully Half...

Some days it's good to run only at half speed in order to recharge to run at full speed, fully. Take some time to slow down and see what comes to mind. This is not an excuse to be lazy, but to deliberately rest and feel what rest feels like.

Respond: Schedule some time off below.

Day 185

Accept ● Forward ● Practice ●

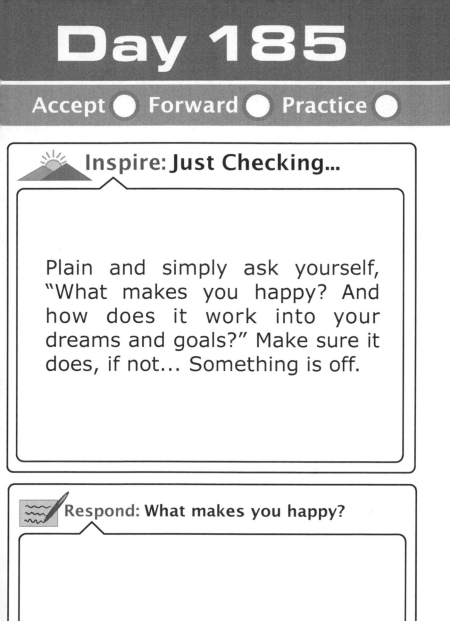

Inspire: Just Checking...

Plain and simply ask yourself, "What makes you happy? And how does it work into your dreams and goals?" Make sure it does, if not... Something is off.

Respond: What makes you happy?

Day 186

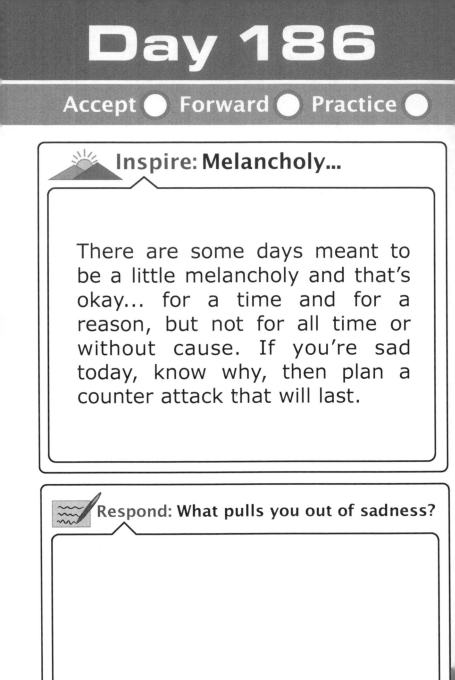

Inspire: Melancholy...

There are some days meant to be a little melancholy and that's okay... for a time and for a reason, but not for all time or without cause. If you're sad today, know why, then plan a counter attack that will last.

Respond: What pulls you out of sadness?

Day 187

Accept ● Forward ● Practice ●

Inspire: Common Link...

On a sheet of paper, list all your best past accomplishments and successes. Then list how you achieved them and find the common link, and duplicate that in your current goals, plans and dreams.

Respond: Bullet point the key words here.

Day 188

Accept ● Forward ● Practice ●

Inspire: Faith that Works...

No matter what your own spiritual beliefs are, have faith in more than just yourself. Give up any thought of going it alone, or achieving with only you in mind. We need more than just the self.

Respond: What do you believe?

Day 189

Inspire: Slow-Mo...

If a plan isn't working... Before giving up, try it again, but this time in "slow-motion". Then, study your ways, note the differences, and speed up gradually, only after grasping what you were missing before.

Respond: What can you do in "Slow-Mo"?

Accept ● Forward ● Practice ●

Inspire: And Again...

Everyday is a new chance to do yesterday better.

Respond: What can you do better today?

Day 191

Accept ● Forward ● Practice ●

Inspire: Too Much Time...

24 hours, 7 days a week should always be enough time for your dreams, goals, and plans, as well as rest and refreshment. If it isn't drop some of the "busy". Learn to be okay with half of what you presently have and find a fullness to life through it.

Respond: What can you drop right now?

Day 192

Accept ● Forward ● Practice ●

Inspire: Stop, Drop, Succeed!

If a project can't succeed without stopping... Stop! And truly succeed... in life. Anything worth doing can and should run at your speed, schedule, and ability.

Respond: What is pushing you too hard?

Day 193

Inspire: Right to be Wrong...

It's okay to be wrong, in fact, sometimes it's the only way to know your dreams are right. Always make sure your intent is to do the right thing and you can never go "wrong". Never stop trying.

Respond: What have you been wrong about?

Day 194

Accept ● Forward ● Practice ●

Inspire: Too Busy to See...

If you're too busy today, then slow down and see all the things that are truly important catch up to you.

Respond: What needs to catch up to you?

Day 195

Accept ● Forward ● Practice ●

Inspire: The Meaning in "It"...

Life. It's about living, not waiting for things you want more than what you presently have. It's about enjoying every part of it, even the parts that are hard. Patience builds endurance, endurance builds strength... Take the time to breathe today and feel where you are at, good or bad, and let go of the desire to control.

Respond: What could you be more patient in?

Day 196

Accept ● Forward ● Practice ●

Inspire: Truest of True...

What is your true desire in achieving your goals? If it is for material gain, it will fall away, if it is to better your world, get ready for things to happen!

Respond: What needs to fall away?

Day 197

Inspire: Who You Are, Again...

A friend told me about a class he took where they would tell you things about yourself you already knew... some people felt the class to be a waste. The others used it to confirm to themselves who they were. Where do you fit in that class?

Respond: What do you know about you?

Day 198

Accept ● Forward ● Practice ●

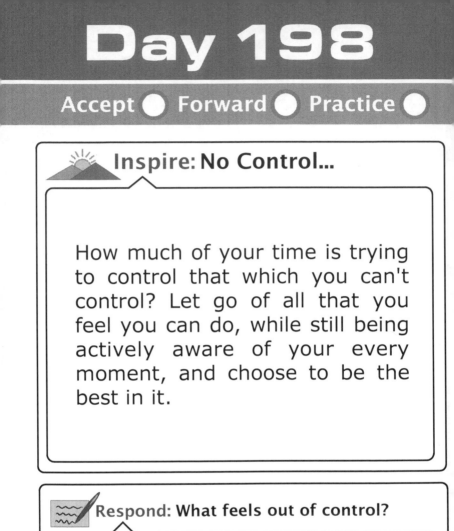

Inspire: No Control...

How much of your time is trying to control that which you can't control? Let go of all that you feel you can do, while still being actively aware of your every moment, and choose to be the best in it.

Respond: What feels out of control?

Day 199

Accept ● Forward ● Practice ●

Inspire: Willing to Walk...

What is it you want most in life? Are you willing to walk away from it, if it isn't good for you? Hold loosely, but embrace all that life offers, and achieve more than you're aware of.

Respond: What can't you walk away from?

Day 200

Accept ● Forward ● Practice ●

Inspire: The Big Question...

What if today is the day that everything in your life changes? Are you ready? Give up the things that bring you down and embrace the gifts you hold inside you! Whether you feel them or not, they're still inside you waiting.

Respond: What has already changed today?

Day 201

Accept ● Forward ● Practice ●

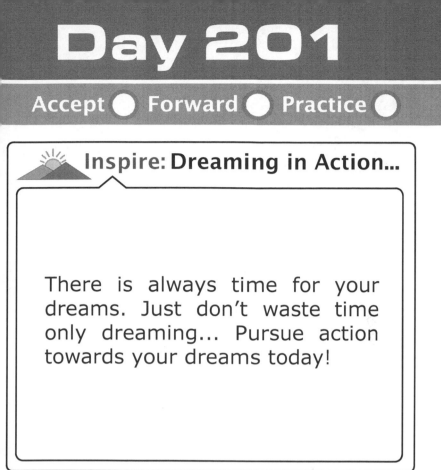

Inspire: Dreaming in Action...

There is always time for your dreams. Just don't waste time only dreaming... Pursue action towards your dreams today!

Respond: What action can you take now?

Day 202

Accept ● Forward ● Practice ●

Inspire: Perceiving You...

What is your perception of you? Where did it come from? Is it one of love, or self-doubt? Know the who, what, where, and when of *you*, and only accept the truth.

Respond: Answer the above questions.

Day 203

Accept ● Forward ● Practice ●

Inspire: Grateful to Be...

What next? How often do you ask yourself or God that question? I seem to ask it minute by minute and still not sure what the answer is, but I am grateful to be able to ask it.

Respond: Who do you ask this of?

Day 204

Inspire: First Things First...

The firsts in our lives prepares us for the seconds... Be open to even a bad first to make a positive second.

Respond: What was better the 2nd time?

Day 205

Accept ● Forward ● Practice ●

Inspire: Stay Together...

What's your greatest desire for life? Have you asked for help to achieve it? We cannot achieve greatness alone. Take a chance and reach out today.

Respond: What have you been trying alone?

Day 206

Inspire: Out with the Bad...

Try to set aside one bad habit for the next 24 hours and see if you think you can do it for another 24. We are what we do, and what we do should be good and good for us.

Respond: List as many bad habits as you can.

Day 207

Accept ● Forward ● Practice ●

Inspire: Why Not Now?

Staying focused takes focus, and practice. Breathe and meditate, pray and think about your goals for at least 5 minutes a day. How about right now?

Respond: What came from your time?

Day 208

Accept ● Forward ● Practice ●

Inspire: By The Way...

I guarantee someone is thinking about you in someway right now. Know that you mean something to this world, and know that your dreams can change it all for more than you!

Respond: Who are you thinking of?

Day 209

Accept ● Forward ● Practice ●

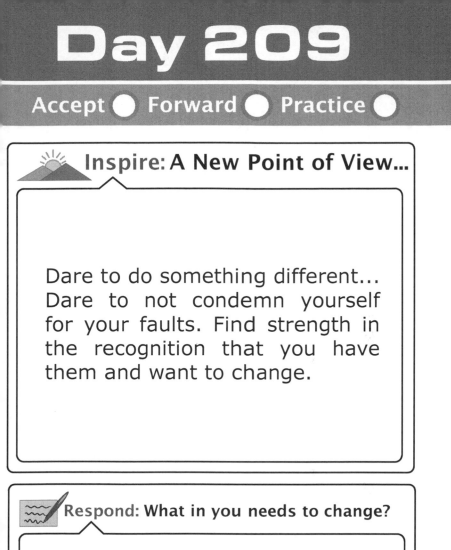

Inspire: A New Point of View...

Dare to do something different... Dare to not condemn yourself for your faults. Find strength in the recognition that you have them and want to change.

Respond: What in you needs to change?

Day 210

Accept ● Forward ● Practice ●

Inspire: A Little Something...

What can you do right now that is small towards your goals, but allows them to move in a big way? Just about everything starts small, it's only when we allow them to grow that they become as big as they need to be to be accomplished. Feed your dream, little by little.

Respond: What small seed is growing?

Day 211

Accept ● Forward ● Practice ●

Inspire: Open 24 Hours...

For the next 24 hours see how much you can accomplish by trying not to accomplish anything other than being your best.

Respond: What keeps you positive?

Day 212

Accept ● Forward ● Practice ●

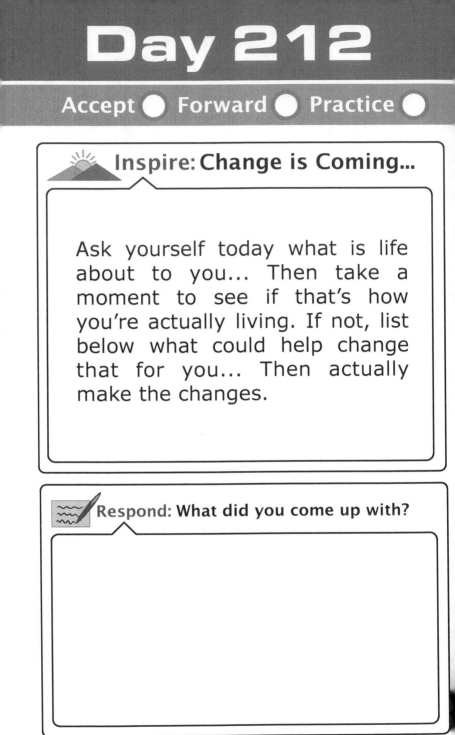

Inspire: Change is Coming...

Ask yourself today what is life about to you... Then take a moment to see if that's how you're actually living. If not, list below what could help change that for you... Then actually make the changes.

Respond: What did you come up with?

Day 213

Inspire: What do We Want?

More often we know what we don't want or need *and* what we unrealistically want and need... But do we strive to find our true or best wants? Do you truly want them? What are they? And what's stopping you from getting them? Can you answer that without blaming anyone? Do your best as blame sends us back to the start.

Respond: List true wants.

Day 214

Accept ● Forward ● Practice ●

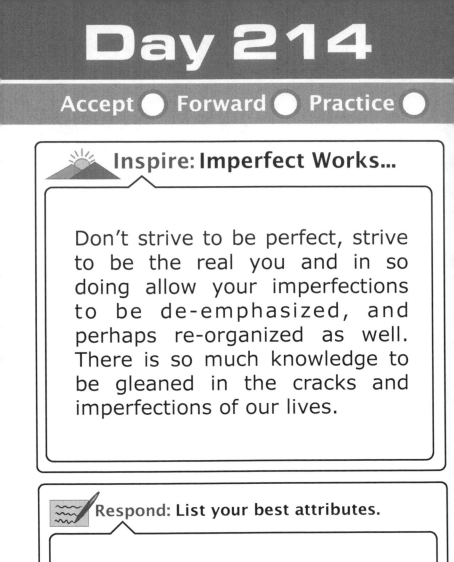

Inspire: Imperfect Works...

Don't strive to be perfect, strive to be the real you and in so doing allow your imperfections to be de-emphasized, and perhaps re-organized as well. There is so much knowledge to be gleaned in the cracks and imperfections of our lives.

Respond: List your best attributes.

Day 215

☼ Inspire: A Thousand Words...

Look in the mirror today and see the unfinished you... And embrace it! Remember, unfinished doesn't mean unlovable, unreliable, or unattainable. There's new layers in you to discover!

✎ Respond: What goal is still out there?

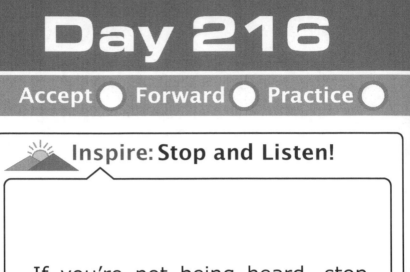

Day 216

Accept ● Forward ● Practice ●

Inspire: Stop and Listen!

If you're not being heard, stop talking and start listening. Learn how to give what you want to get.

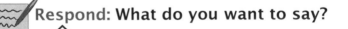

Respond: What do you want to say?

Day 217

Accept ● Forward ● Practice ●

Inspire: Keep Striving...

Push through to the end of each day knowing you are adding to the greater goal of your life's work! Remember, even a great life can't be without some mediocre moments. They help build patience, which is one of the greatest attributes to have.

Respond: What bores you, and why?

Day 218

Accept ● Forward ● Practice ●

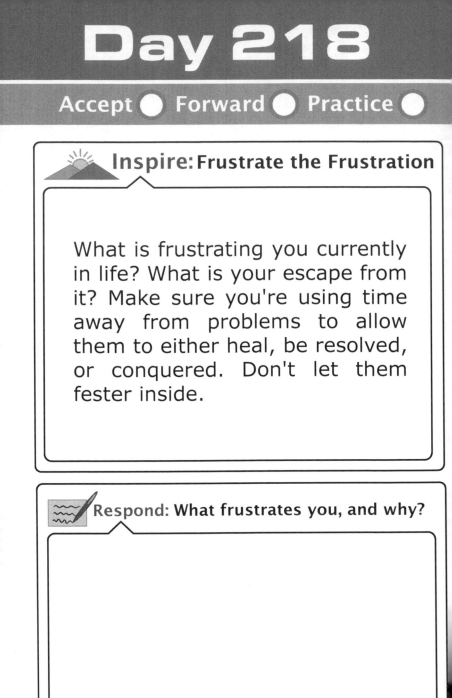

Inspire: Frustrate the Frustration

What is frustrating you currently in life? What is your escape from it? Make sure you're using time away from problems to allow them to either heal, be resolved, or conquered. Don't let them fester inside.

Respond: What frustrates you, and why?

Day 219

Inspire: Fully Known...

Fulfillment is not about having everything you desire, it's about enjoying the journey of life. Seek to desire everything you already have, and enjoy the gifts that are already in and a part of you and your life.

Respond: What is awesome in your life?

Day 220

Accept ● Forward ● Practice ○

Inspire: Good Habits...

We've learned to brush our teeth and wash our hands several times in a day, can we do the same with remembering our goals and following through on them?

Respond: What are your goals today?

Day 221

Accept ● Forward ● Practice ●

Inspire: On My Mind...

As I sit here, I think and pray about what I can write to you. Today the one thing that I really think you may need to hear is... Today matters, *you* matter. You are important to the whole picture! Have a blessed day!

Respond: Write what you want.

Day 222

Inspire: Plain Truth...

Above all things in your life, seek truth, and the truth will find you. Just be ready for it and willing to accept it no matter what it is, and how far from your current belief or thoughts it might be.

Respond: Do you know real truth?

Day 223

Inspire: Ageless Thinking...

No matter how old we are... There are always new things inside us, waiting to be born. Just remember you're never too old to give in to them and let them live.

Respond: What have you learned lately?

Day 224

Inspire: Ready and Willing...

To live full and free, live willing and able to give up the will to think you know everything and can do it all on your own. Our *own* will can only take us so far.

Respond: What are you trying to control?

Day 225

Accept ● Forward ● Practice ●

Inspire: Know Your Poison...

Ask yourself, can I walk away from the things that make me angry? If not, list below what makes you angry, memorize them (but don't stew in them) so when they get close to you, you can be aware and begin moving away before it gets triggered.

Respond: What makes you angry?

Day 226

Accept ● Forward ● Practice ●

Inspire: As it Happens...

Take a moment to live what you're doing right at this moment. No matter your situation, living it fully will bring you more knowledge about it and allow you to grow in your experiences.

Respond: What are you going through?

Day 227

Accept ● Forward ● Practice ●

Inspire: Thank You Note...

Take a moment to thank some-one in the next 24 hours that has been special to you that may not know it; it will make you both feel awesome!

Respond: How does it feel to be loved?

Day 228

Inspire: Willing and Able...

Be honest and true no matter what in life, and stand firm that truth will always win out in the end. But also know you don't know when it ends, so just be willing.

Respond: How does truth affect you?

Day 229

Accept ● Forward ● Practice ●

Inspire: Love these Times...

Some days you can accomplish more in the long term by applying yourself to only one simple task.

Respond: Write down the little things.

Day 230

Accept ● Forward ● Practice ●

Inspire: Faultless in Truth...

Admit fault when you're in the wrong and allow truth to permeate your life. It may set an example that is picked up by others or it may not, but the truth will always set you free.

Respond: How does the truth feel?

Day 231

Accept ● Forward ● Practice ●

Inspire: Stress the Distress...

Compile a list of what stresses you out and read it out loud each day... BUT, make sure you say along with it, "I will conquer..." or "...does not phase me, I will overcome this." Do it often and see it's hold release.

Respond: What stresses you out?

Day 232

Accept ● Forward ● Practice ●

Inspire: Destined to Believe...

If you believe in destiny, believe also in the best one for you. You are loved, you are able, no matter what.

Respond: What are you destined for?

Day 233

Accept ● Forward ● Practice ●

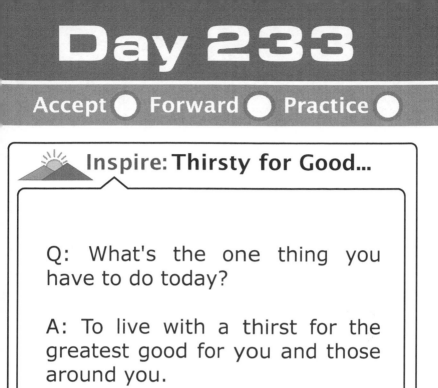

Inspire: Thirsty for Good...

Q: What's the one thing you have to do today?

A: To live with a thirst for the greatest good for you and those around you.

Respond: What would help someone today?

Day 234

Accept ● Forward ● Practice ●

Inspire: Forget & Forgive...

Is there someone you need to forgive today? You will be set free by letting go of the anger, frustrations, and hurt. Let it go, and live!

Respond: Who have you not forgiven?

Day 235

Accept ● Forward ● Practice ●

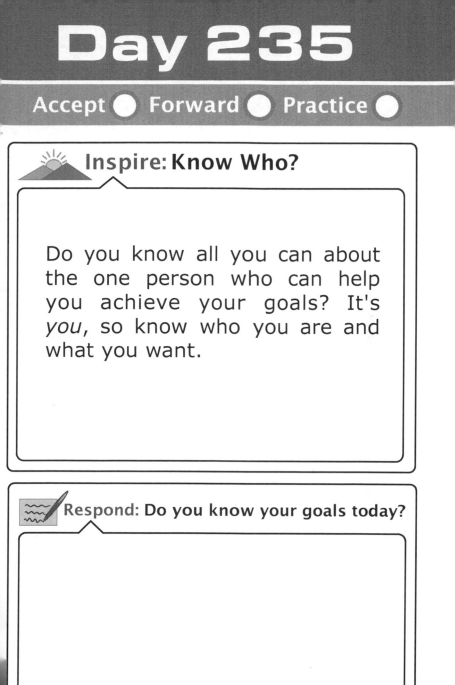

Inspire: Know Who?

Do you know all you can about the one person who can help you achieve your goals? It's *you*, so know who you are and what you want.

Respond: Do you know your goals today?

Day 236

Accept ● Forward ● Practice ●

Inspire: The Right Start...

Do your best to start your day with something you're good at. It will set a base and show that you have a right to be confident in all you do.

Respond: List things to start today with.

Accept ● Forward ● Practice ●

☀ Inspire: **Perfectly Imperfect...**

Today is a perfect day to be imperfect. Know that you can't do everything, but the things you can do can affect others positively, so do them the best you can, and that will be good enough.

✎ Respond: **What can you do today?**

Day 238

Inspire: Bigger Dreams...

When your dreams get too big for your current life, then you know you're onto something! Keep moving forward, and your life will grow into your new confidence.

Respond: What dream seems too big?

Day 239

Accept ● Forward ● Practice ●

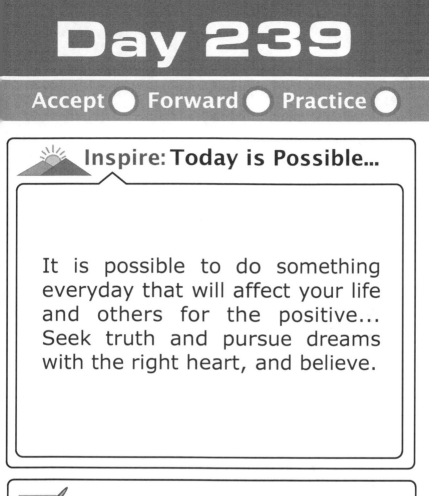

Inspire: Today is Possible...

It is possible to do something everyday that will affect your life and others for the positive... Seek truth and pursue dreams with the right heart, and believe.

Respond: What positives have you done?

Day 240

Inspire: Expect to Accept...

This life is made to live. Details will come and go, situations will too, but a heart set on a consistent goal of "living" will bring you the truth. Seek truth today. And be ready to accept it when it comes, even if it's not what you expected.

Respond: What details bog you down?

Day 241

Inspire: Life in Focus...

Focus on what makes you focus. Write a list of all the things that help you, and when you're feeling scattered go to the list and do what helps you stay centered.

Respond: List what helps you focus.

Day 242

Accept ● Forward ● Practice ●

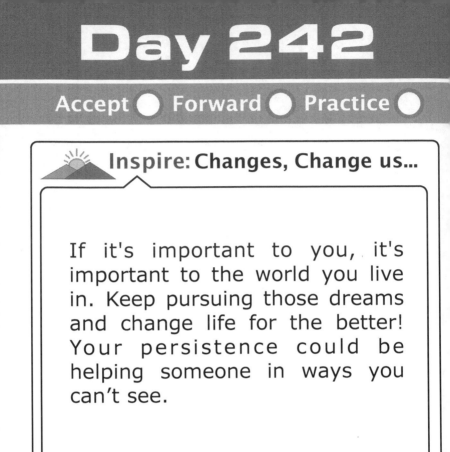

Inspire: Changes, Change us...

If it's important to you, it's important to the world you live in. Keep pursuing those dreams and change life for the better! Your persistence could be helping someone in ways you can't see.

Respond: List some recent accomplishments.

Day 243

Accept ● Forward ● Practice ●

Inspire: Choose Wisely...

Life can be about choices... if you choose it to be. Be open to options and choose which one benefits you and others the most.

Respond: Do choices bother you? Why?

Accept ● Forward ● Practice ●

Inspire: Little Voice, Big Trouble...

How often do you cut yourself some slack, and how often do you let that little voice in that says not to? Don't cut the little voice any, let it go. Move forward and accept your past mistakes.

Respond: What lies are you accepting?

Day 245

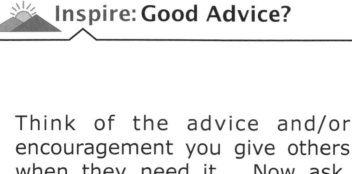

Inspire: Good Advice?

Think of the advice and/or encouragement you give others when they need it... Now ask, are you applying it to yourself as well? You can and should.

Respond: What advice would you give you?

Day 246

Inspire: What is Truth?

Believe your life is what you want it to be and watch what happens! Start right now. List what you want from life and then vocalize it throughout the day. "My life is awesome, here's why..." Keep saying and seeing the good, and it will come.

 Respond: What do you want life to be?

Day 247

Accept ● Forward ● Practice ●

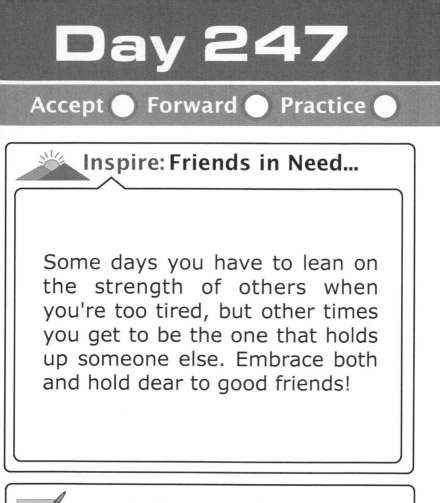

Inspire: Friends in Need...

Some days you have to lean on the strength of others when you're too tired, but other times you get to be the one that holds up someone else. Embrace both and hold dear to good friends!

Respond: Who are your friends?

Day 248

Inspire: Opposition Arises...

Yes, you will be challenged, yes, you will be opposed at times, yes, it will be hard, but, YES, YOU CAN PURSUE and ACHIEVE YOUR DREAMS! Use all of your life to create the best life.

Respond: What is opposing you today?

Day 249

Accept ● Forward ● Practice ●

Inspire: First Off, First Off...

What do you have to do today and what can wait? Even if you don't want to, even if it's really hard, boring or not what you want, but it is best for you in the long run... Do that first!

Respond: What should you do first today?

Day 250

Accept ● Forward ● Practice ●

Inspire: Build Better Belief...

Just as the body recovers and rebuilds after injury or illness, we must do the same with our daily choices in life and in turn, create a strong immune system that can defeat thoughts of failure or stagnation. Believe in the best for you and those around you!

Respond: How can you build more belief?

Inspire: Seeing it Through...

Remember life's not always what we want or expect, but it's what we do with it that matters. Find something that matters to you today and see it through to the end.

Respond: What can you finish today?

Day 252

Inspire: Give & Receive...

Sometimes it's easy to see someone else's potential and not our own. Let someone know today what you see in them and perhaps you might get the same back.

Respond: Where's your potential?

Day 253

Accept ● Forward ● Practice ●

Inspire: The Positive Core...

What is the core belief you hold and how can you strengthen it with each breath? By only taking in positive and leaving the negative thoughts, words, and deeds behind. When a negative comes in today, breathe it out with a positive and see what happens.

Respond: List some positives to use today.

Day 254

Accept ● Forward ● Practice ●

Inspire: What do I See?

IT'S HAPPENING RIGHT NOW! YOUR LIFE!! So live it. Right now, stop, look around, and say aloud all the good you see, and then be thankful for it. Have a blessed day.

Respond: What did you see?

Day 255

Accept ● Forward ● Practice ●

Inspire: Laugh it Off...

Today the second a negative happens, instantly smile, or laugh, and begin retraining yourself to see it as just another part of life that is manageable, and that you're capable of handling it. How we react is a big part of what lives in us.

Respond: Write, "I am capable of change."

Day 256

Accept ● Forward ● Practice ●

Inspire: To Do, Today...

Ask yourself, "What do I really want to do today?" Then write down the various steps that come to mind to make it happen, then... get busy! If you can achieve even a fraction of it, you've achieved more than doing nothing about it.

Respond: Write it down, make it happen.

Day 257

Accept ● Forward ● Practice ●

Inspire: Help You, Help Me...

How are you looking at yourself and others today? Equally? Are you placing them higher than you or worse, you higher than them? Remember to see the world through your neighbor's eyes as well, and know we're all just trying to make it through to something better.

Respond: Who needs your support today?

Day 258

Accept ● Forward ● Practice ●

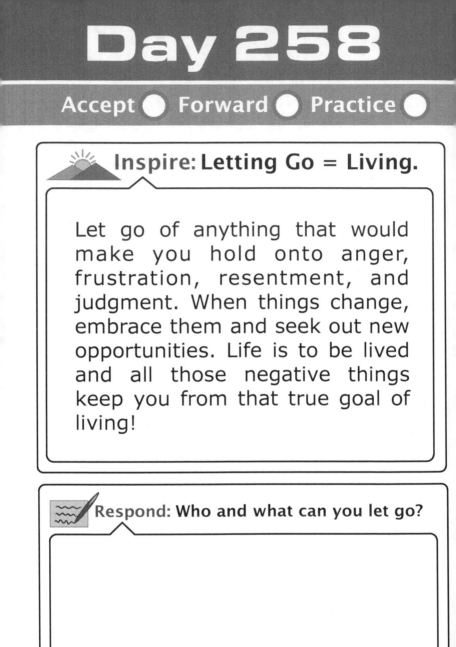

Inspire: Letting Go = Living.

Let go of anything that would make you hold onto anger, frustration, resentment, and judgment. When things change, embrace them and seek out new opportunities. Life is to be lived and all those negative things keep you from that true goal of living!

Respond: Who and what can you let go?

Day 259

Accept ● Forward ● Practice ●

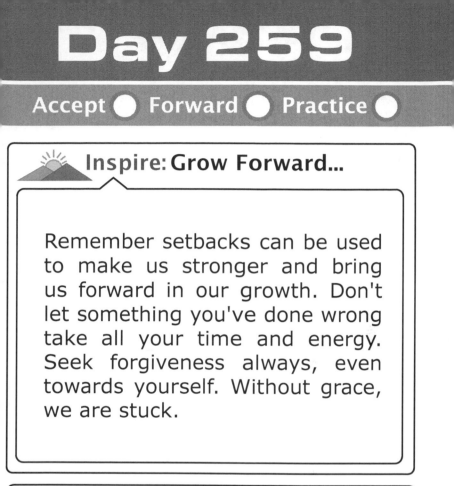

Inspire: Grow Forward...

Remember setbacks can be used to make us stronger and bring us forward in our growth. Don't let something you've done wrong take all your time and energy. Seek forgiveness always, even towards yourself. Without grace, we are stuck.

Respond: Where can you give you grace?

Day 260

Accept ● Forward ● Practice ●

Inspire: Future's So Bright...

It's a new day, and it's a new chance to see things in a new way. Look with confidence towards your future, and you will find confidence waiting for you.

Respond: What're you looking forward to?

Day 261

Accept ● Forward ● Practice ●

Inspire: I Think You Can...

That which you have set before you is not impossible! It's achievable when you believe and never give up! Yes, I have said it over and again, but are you believing it yet? You can! I believe in you!

Respond: What can you achieve?

Day 262

Accept ● Forward ● Practice ●

Inspire: You In Action...

Remember, it's up to you to put your dreams into action! You can, if you do! Never give up, and find that you'll never want to.

Respond: What is inspiring you today?

Day 263

Accept ● Forward ● Practice ●

Inspire: Living Stronger...

If it is something you don't want to do, there's a good chance it needs to get done. Doing it will make you stronger and more able to do all things more effectively. Do it right after finishing this page.

Respond: What don't you want to do?

Day 264

Accept ● Forward ● Practice ●

Inspire: Today, Achieved...

Choose to believe today that you can achieve all that you set out to. When the day is done reflect on all you accomplished. Knowing that what wasn't can be accomplished tomorrow. The goal is to be positive about your actions and your belief in achieving your goals.

Respond: Write "I can accomplish..."

Day 265

Accept ● Forward ● Practice ●

Inspire: On Your Mark...

It's a new day, it's a new chance to pursue new things in a new way! Be renewed! Put away the negative thoughts, complaints, or grumblings and know that you can start over right this second. The slate is clean... GO!

Respond: Write, "Today I will..."

Day 266

 **Inspire: Remember to Remind...**

Throughout the day, tell yourself that you can and will achieve the best in your life. It's these little reminders that begin to stick and make a big difference in the long run! I believe you can do it! Now it's your turn!

Respond: Write, then say, "I can do it!"

Day 267

Accept ● Forward ● Practice ●

Inspire: A Pep Talk...

I can't say, "I can't". I won't say, "I won't". I will say, "I will..." Believe you can, and know you will. Keep going, it gets easier.

Respond: Write whatever you want.

Day 268

Accept ● Forward ● Practice ○

Inspire: I Think You Can...

Whether your day started the way you planned or not, whether you are happy or sad, encouraged or discouraged, the moments continue on, which means there is always a chance to change; and believe that someone else (me) knows you can turn it around.

Respond: How can you help you?

Day 269

Accept ● Forward ● Practice ●

Inspire: Wrong But Right...

Whenever I think I'm right about something, I always have to ask myself, "Is it right, just for me, or for others too?" The greatest gift you can give in an argument with someone is to be willing to be wrong and admit it if you are. Tough stuff, I know, but it truly matters.

Respond: Write & say, "It's ok to be wrong."

Day 270

Inspire: Live Life and Live...

Life is beautiful if you take the time to enjoy it with all your senses. Look at a tree, feel the air breezing past you, smell your next meal, listen to the sound of your surroundings. Find the best parts of it all and remember them. Then when you're stressed, recall them! It works!

Respond: What's your favorite memory?

Day 271

Accept ● Forward ● Practice ●

Inspire: No Matter What...

Let the work you do be an extension of your talents and abilities, not just something to pay the bills. No matter what you're doing, do it as though it's the best job in the world. Eventually, what you truly desire can become that much more attainable through this positive outlook.

Respond: What's the best of what you do?

Day 272

Inspire: Don't Let Them In...

Give up the parts of you that do nothing positive for you or anyone else. It's easy to spot them; they're the ones that come upon you fast and leave no joy when you do them.

Respond: Write, "I will give up..."

Day 273

Accept ● Forward ● Practice ●

 **Inspire: Peace Within...**

Sometimes it's hard to find peace, but know that it is within your own heart, you just have to let it live through you. Take some time today to search for the peace in you.

Respond: Write & say, "I will seek peace".

Day 274

Accept ● Forward ● Practice ●

Inspire: Give Up To Get Up...

What are you willing to give up to achieve more in life? There are many habits, traits, even people in our lives that are detrimental to our growth. Always be willing to look deeper at yourself and find the parts that aren't needed, and try giving them up.

Respond: What's holding you back?

Day 275

Accept ● Forward ● Practice ●

Inspire: Back to the Future...

We should always be looking upwards (positively) whether we look backwards or forwards. Our past mistakes can help our future successes.

Respond: What "mistake" helped you?

Day 276

Accept ● Forward ● Practice ●

Inspire: A Long Journey...

Remember, it's not impossible to do what you set out to, but it may be tough at times. Endure! It's worth it! Practice patience in the enduring and remind yourself this is part of the journey.

Respond: What's the roughest part today?

Day 277

Accept ● Forward ● Practice ●

 **Inspire: Bigger Picture...**

The bigger picture should always be your goal. Keep pushing forward, all the while structuring your plans. The organization gets easier when you remind yourself why you're doing it.

Respond: What's your bigger picture?

Inspire: The Good Fight...

Some days are tougher than others to stay positive. That's when you have to fight through it! Don't waste your time and energy being negative. Life is full of positives, find them today and feel alive!

Respond: What are you fighting against?

Day 279

Accept ● Forward ● Practice ●

Inspire: Spare Change...

I find usually nowadays, when I pass someone on the street and say, "Hi", they usually say nothing and look away. Strange how we are that alone surrounded by each other. Take a risk and be the one that reaches out today, no matter the outcome. You stretched yourself and your boundaries, that's good change!

Respond: Is it hard to change? Why?

Day 280

Accept ● Forward ● Practice ●

Inspire: Dream of Reality...

If you're gonna "Day Dream" dream of things that are possible and then set plans to achieve them! You can do it! Many before you have; the path is laid, you can succeed!

Respond: What are you dreaming of today?

Day 281

Accept ● Forward ● Practice ●

Inspire: You See You...

Do you know what you think about you? If not, try writing it down. It may reveal things you didn't think you thought and show you where you need to grow, and what you need to embrace. It's okay to like YOU.

Respond: What do you think about you?

Day 282

Accept ● Forward ● Practice ●

Inspire: Do Over...

Take all the things that are bugging you right now... and let go of them... RIGHT NOW! You can free yourself and start fresh with a positive attitude each day! Believe. Clear your mind, breathe, and start over.

Respond: What do you love?

Day 283

Inspire: All New, All Now...

It's not just a new day, it's a chance to do new things in a moment that has never existed before! Do something awesome! See it inspire you and others!

Respond: What's your motivation?

Day 284

Accept ● Forward ● Practice ●

Inspire: The Blink of an Eye...

In a second you can change your day, or even your life, by deciding to focus on what you CAN do, not what you can't.

Respond: What are you really good at?

Day 285

Accept ● Forward ● Practice ●

Inspire: More and More...

All we strive for, all we hope for, all we work for, should always make us know more and in so doing we truly do become more.

Respond: Write down and see your goal.

Day 286

Accept ● Forward ● Practice ●

Inspire: Who Are You?

Persistence can be to your advantage or disadvantage. Pursue what you're meant for, admit to chasing what isn't for you, and let it go.

Respond: What do you need to let go of?

Day 287

Accept ● Forward ● Practice ●

Inspire: Surprised by Surprise...

Life will always throw surprises your way. Know that. In fact, say it out loud to accept it. Then, live like they are part of the plan and they won't surprise you as much, and will be easier to dismiss.

Respond: How do you react to surprises?

Day 288

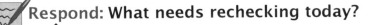 Inspire: **Confirm not Conform...**

It's possible to double check your motives and self without becoming obsessive about it. To go back and confirm what you're doing is right can reaffirm and even rejuvenate a goal or plan. Keep your paths straight, follow the good and know your motives.

Respond: **What needs rechecking today?**

Day 289

Inspire: Decide to Accept...

When you assert yourself do you later feel guilty or over think it? Or fear others don't like you for it? Stop! Accept your decisions; they help show *us* who *we* are. Being decisive is a vital part of success!

Respond: List your best decisions.

Day 290

Accept ● Forward ● Practice ●

Inspire: You Are Enough...

Don't let anyone put you down... including yourself! This one can slip through the cracks too often. Don't allow inner conflict about you to exist. Know who you are, what you are striving for, and that your efforts are good enough and moving you forward.

Respond: What do you like about you?

Day 291

Inspire: Gone for Good...

What are you holding onto today that you should let go of? Write it down on a piece of paper. See it for what it is (or was), then destroy the paper and move on! We cannot change the past, but we can accept it as something that happened, knowing that many wonderful things happen as well.

Respond: Write down a good memory.

Day 292

Accept ● Forward ● Practice ●

Inspire: Simply Respond...

Simplify your responses today and watch your time grow!

Respond: List some goals for today.

Day 293

Accept ● Forward ● Practice ●

Inspire: Simply Smile...

When you find yourself doing nothing in those little moments, smile and do something bigger than it may seem. Happiness is a necessity!

Respond: What makes you smile?

Day 294

Inspire: Stick to It...

No matter what tries to distract you today... Stay the course! Stick to your plans, and find peace.

Respond: What's your plan today?

Day 295

Accept ● Forward ● Practice ●

Inspire: Feeling for a Friend...

Sometimes the best thing we can be to a friend in need is a set of ears to listen, arms to hold them, or to say a prayer for them when they can't get themselves to. Be there for someone today.

Respond: Are there others that need you?

Day 296

Accept ● Forward ● Practice ●

Inspire: Seek Truthfully...

Seek truth today and it will find you. Just be ready to face it when it does, and to always give it to others as well. Truth is a great healer.

Respond: Who do you need to tell the truth?

Day 297

Accept ● Forward ● Practice ●

Inspire: What's Next?

There are journeys ahead that you are not aware of, but you can be prepared for them by accepting that all roads lead to a stronger you!

Respond: How can you react to change?

Day 298

Accept ● Forward ● Practice ●

Inspire: Setting Truth Free...

Rest in truth. And know that it doesn't work hard to be, it just is. No matter how people may try to change it. Truth is truth, period.

Respond: What is true in your life?

Day 299

Accept ● Forward ● Practice ●

 Inspire: **Powerful Pondering...**

Remember as many negatives there are to sit and ponder there are just as many positives. Think about the good you can accomplish in your life, then pursue! Start right now...

Respond: **What is good to go after?**

Day 300

Inspire: Simply More...

Keep it simple today. Don't accept more than you can accomplish. Then at the end of the day see how much more you achieved. And make note of it below.

Respond: What happened today?

Day 301

Accept ● Forward ● Practice ●

Inspire: Positive Strength...

We can find strength in difficulties. Stay positive no matter what surrounds you and watch what surrounds you change for the positive. It truly works!

Respond: When have you seen this work?

Day 302

Accept ● Forward ● Practice ●

Inspire: Feel the Facts...

Feelings are always present, just make sure they don't override the facts when dealing with others.

Respond: How do you handle feelings?

Day 303

Accept ● Forward ● Practice ●

Inspire: Know Your Enemy...

List what makes you angry, frustrated, irritable. That way you know what to avoid. Conquer the negative by understanding how it affects you and committing to stay away from it.

Respond: What gets to you?

Day 304

Accept ● Forward ● Practice ●

Inspire: Destination, Control...

It's not about controlling your destiny, it's about letting go of what is controlling you, and in turn, allowing your thoughts to be destined for greatness!

Respond: What is out of control in you?

Day 305

Accept ● Forward ● Practice ●

☀ Inspire: **Nothing Wasted...**

Nothing you're experiencing is wasted, if you believe it's for the bigger picture of your life. Grab hold and live it all! Even the tough parts can become a blessing!

✎ Respond: **List some past blessings.**

Day 306

Accept ● Forward ● Practice ○

Inspire: Right? or Wrong?

Remember no matter how certain we are, there is always another person's perspective. Seek balance in what you do and always be willing to be wrong.

Respond: Who can you learn from?

Day 307

Accept ● Forward ● Practice ●

Inspire: New to You...

There may be "nothing new under the sun", but there is plenty we can learn that's new to us. Be ready to learn today!

Respond: What "new" can you seek today?

Day 308

Accept ● Forward ● Practice ●

 **Inspire: Be Here and Hear...**

Be present, and listen to all that is said to you, good and bad, and use it all for your betterment! Seek wisdom, knowledge, and understanding. They are indispensable to a life that is true.

Respond: Where do you find truth?

Day 309

Accept ● Forward ● Practice ●

Inspire: Giving not to Get...

It's easy to be selfish, much harder to be selfless. Give of your talents today! Do for more than just you and feel the warmth of giving.

Respond: What can you give today?

Day 310

Accept ● Forward ● Practice ●

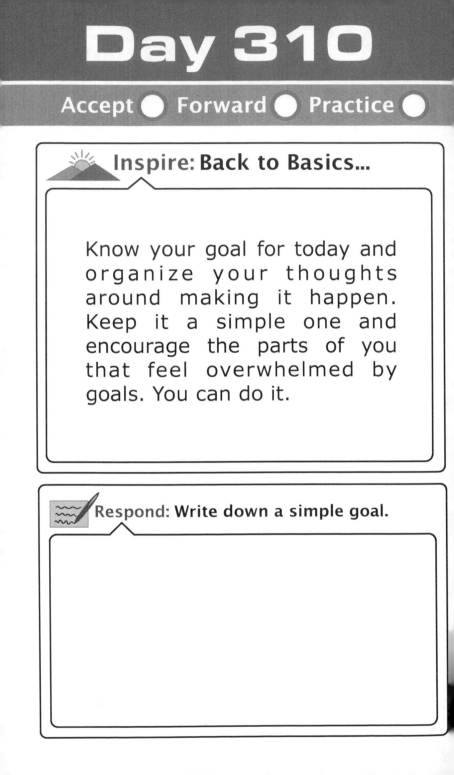

Inspire: Back to Basics...

Know your goal for today and organize your thoughts around making it happen. Keep it a simple one and encourage the parts of you that feel overwhelmed by goals. You can do it.

Respond: Write down a simple goal.

Day 311

Accept ● Forward ● Practice ●

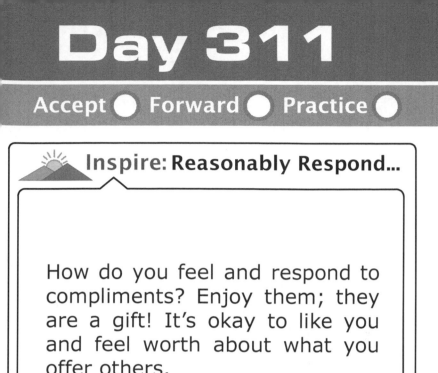

Inspire: Reasonably Respond...

How do you feel and respond to compliments? Enjoy them; they are a gift! It's okay to like you and feel worth about what you offer others.

Respond: How do compliments feel?

Day 312

Inspire: K(no)w Challenge...

What is challenging you today? It could be there to make you stronger, so embrace it, and do your best to conquer it the best you can. And say aloud now that you can!

Respond: Write some positives about it.

Day 313

Inspire: Worry... Away...

Whatever you're worrying about today can become either a wall or speed bump in your life, depending on how you approach it. It may require a slow speed, but you can get over it!

Respond: Where can you slow down?

Day 314

Accept ● Forward ● Practice ○

☀ Inspire: Laugh, Cry, Feel...

Find a moment to genuinely laugh today. Read a joke or funny story, watch a funny clip on-line, remember a past situation that made you laugh... to the point of tears. It will heal you if you let it, and you will feel the difference!

✎ Respond: Who can you share laughs with?

Day 315

Accept ● Forward ● Practice ●

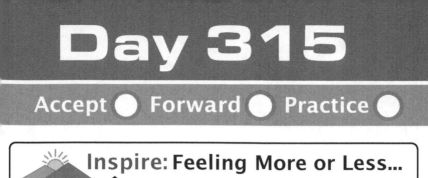 **Inspire: Feeling More or Less...**

This life is full of many things you *feel* you have to do... But what is it that you can do today that will help you feel accomplished? Truly think about it and find answers.

 **Respond: What are you feeling right now?**

Day 316

Inspire: Struggle vs Growth...

Yes, you more than likely will hit a struggle of some type today, but will you use it to grow or to complain? Think of it as growing pains and rejoice in all that will come from it.

Respond: Where are you growing today?

Day 317

Accept ● Forward ● Practice ●

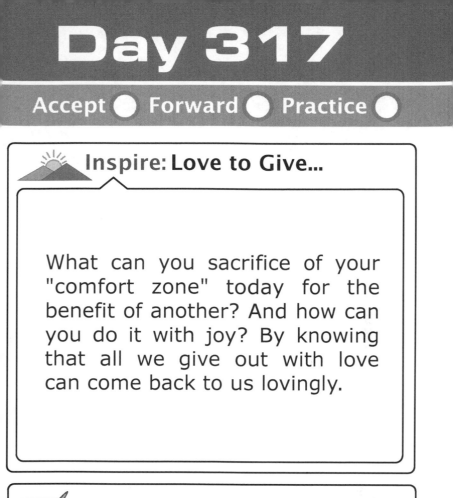

Inspire: Love to Give...

What can you sacrifice of your "comfort zone" today for the benefit of another? And how can you do it with joy? By knowing that all we give out with love can come back to us lovingly.

Respond: When did love come back to you?

Day 318

Accept ● Forward ● Practice ●

Inspire: Worth Repeating...

I've said it before, but it's worth reminding us both... Know what you're good at... AND what you're NOT good at. It matters when accomplishing goals!

Respond: Why does it matter?

Day 319

Accept ● Forward ● Practice ●

 **Inspire: Direct Direction...**

When you have direction in life, you have a way to direct your creativity. Be flexible in how you learn, yet firm in what you're learning! Know your goals, stick to them!

Respond: What have you learned so far?

Day 320

Accept ● Forward ● Practice ●

Inspire: Better? You Bet!

You can do something everyday of your life to make someone else or others happy, but it has to start with a desire to please you as well. Goodness should work for all involved.

Respond: How does it feel to do for you?

Day 321

Accept ● Forward ● Practice ●

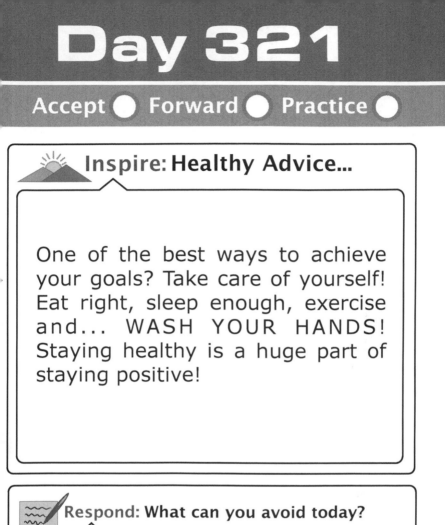

Inspire: Healthy Advice...

One of the best ways to achieve your goals? Take care of yourself! Eat right, sleep enough, exercise and... WASH YOUR HANDS! Staying healthy is a huge part of staying positive!

Respond: What can you avoid today?

Day 322

Accept ● Forward ● Practice ●

Inspire: Passionate Belief...

Passion is important, but understanding and knowledge of why we believe what we believe shows wisdom. Know what you believe... *Then* be passionate about it!

Respond: What are your core beliefs?

Day 323

Accept ● Forward ● Practice ●

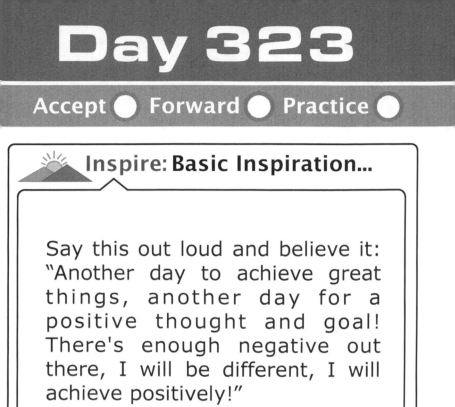

Inspire: Basic Inspiration...

Say this out loud and believe it: "Another day to achieve great things, another day for a positive thought and goal! There's enough negative out there, I will be different, I will achieve positively!"

Respond: What can you add to the above?

Day 324

Accept ● Forward ● Practice ●

Inspire: Good & Contagious...

Remember to grab life and shake it up today! You can make a difference in the lives around you by showing them your love and happiness! To walk into situations today happy, is to give an important gift to others.

Respond: Who needs your happiness?

Day 325

Accept ● Forward ● Practice ●

Inspire: Looking Back...

Remember to look back from time to time in life on all you've accomplished. I bet you've done more than you thought, and affected more people in ways you may never see. Look back through this book and see some results!

Respond: Where have you surprised you?

Day 326

Accept ● Forward ● Practice ●

Inspire: A New Path...

It's a great day to be on a new path! Put away the word "negative" and reinvigorate yourself with the "positive"! Say, aloud, "I am moving towards my goals, and achieving good!"

Respond: How does it feel to do good?

Day 327

Accept ● Forward ● Practice ●

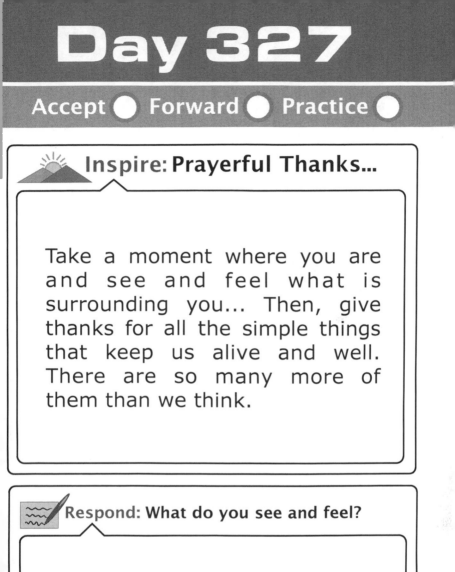

Inspire: Prayerful Thanks...

Take a moment where you are and see and feel what is surrounding you... Then, give thanks for all the simple things that keep us alive and well. There are so many more of them than we think.

Respond: What do you see and feel?

Day 328

Accept ● Forward ● Practice ●

Inspire: Count the Ways...

How many things were "unachievable" at some point in your life that are now second nature to you? There's more than you think and more inside you to come. Accomplishments are behind and ahead of you, rejoice in them all!

Respond: List some past "Unachievables".

Day 329

Accept ● Forward ● Practice ●

Inspire: Brain On...

They say it's good to switch up your hands while doing random tasks from time to time to keep the other side of your brain active. Today, switch up the part of your brain that wants to go negative by only feeding it positives and feel the difference!

Respond: List some positives in your life.

Day 330

Accept ● Forward ● Practice ●

Inspire: Fail Safe...

Don't allow guilt to fill you up when you fail at being positive. Every second of every day is a new chance to begin a positive thought, and the past ones are part of the learning process. It may take time, but you will get it!

Respond: List some favorite positives.

Day 331

Inspire: Say it, Believe it...

Say the following today, "Today is a new day. All things in my life can be new today, I believe it and will grab hold of it by staying focused on it. Life is good!" It may seem goofy, but it does help to say these things and believe them.

Respond: Write your own version to say.

Day 332

Accept ● Forward ● Practice ○

Inspire: Know What You Know...

Sometimes it's what we haven't said that speaks volumes. Make sure you are honest with anyone you're in conflict with and always know what you believe. If you don't know, ask yourself what you believe and why? Then always be ready to share it.

Respond: What are your core beliefs?

Day 333

Accept ● Forward ● Practice ●

Inspire: High Hopes...

Ants create mountains by moving a single piece of sand at a time. Can you have the patience and endurance of the ant? Resting in the knowledge that even the smallest movements forward are helping you achieve the biggest goals?

Respond: Where can you be more patient?

Day 334

Accept ● Forward ● Practice ●

Inspire: Stay the Course...

Whatever you do today, do it with your best foot forward and the best intentions. No matter if others see it or appreciate it, you will know that you stayed the course, and in so doing, will help you in the long term more than you can imagine.

Respond: How does it feel to do good?

Day 335

Accept ● Forward ● Practice ●

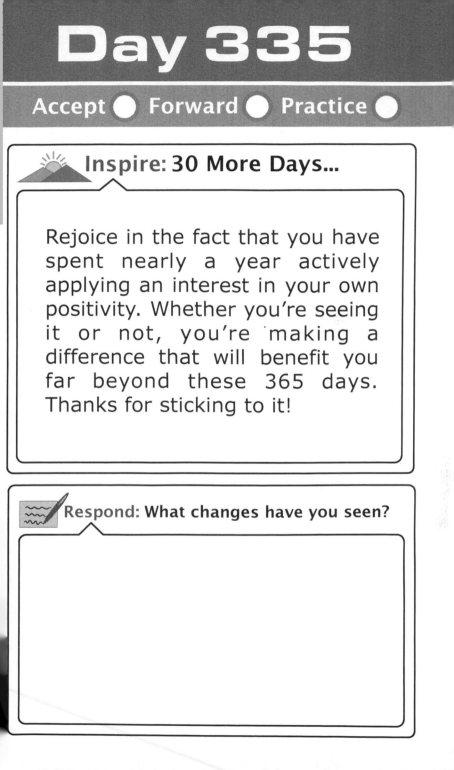

Inspire: 30 More Days...

Rejoice in the fact that you have spent nearly a year actively applying an interest in your own positivity. Whether you're seeing it or not, you're making a difference that will benefit you far beyond these 365 days. Thanks for sticking to it!

Respond: What changes have you seen?

Day 336

Inspire: Real Negativity...

You can be "real" with your closest friends and family without turning to negative words. Sometimes we're more negative with loved ones because we think we're letting our guard down. But positivity is contagious. Help each other stay positive by speaking positively.

Respond: Who needs your positivity?

Day 337

Accept ● Forward ● Practice ●

Inspire: Inspiration is Key...

Keep your mind refreshed by reading things that are positive. In fact, seek them out. Stories of success, biographies of your favorite people or innovators. I find refreshment in The Psalms and Proverbs, in art and poetry. It all reminds us of beauty and what can be achieved when we stay focused.

Respond: What would you like to read?

Day 338

Accept ● Forward ● Practice ●

Inspire: Breathe In, Stay Out...

If weather permits, go outside for an extended length and breathe in the real life air of a park, beach, or natural area. If you really want to get crazy, go bare foot for awhile and feel even more real!

Respond: Where's your favorite place?

Day 339

Accept ● Forward ● Practice ●

Inspire: See Through You...

Find pictures of you that are from a different perspective than what you see when you look in the mirror. Knowing how others see us helps us to see more fully who we are. Also, do your best to enjoy what you see. Self esteem is important to a dream fulfilled.

Respond: What do you like about you?

Day 340

Accept ● Forward ● Practice ●

Inspire: Certain Sleep...

How do you sleep? If poorly, change up what you do before going to bed. No food, no computer, or TV. Simply unplug and take some time to feel and relax. True rest allows for true clarity about dreams and goals. You can change your sleep for the better.

Respond: What can change before bed?

Day 341

Accept ● Forward ● Practice ●

Inspire: Give and Get...

Give someone something beautiful and unexpected today. It could be as simple as a note expressing your true feelings about them... and it could even be *you* that needs to hear this from you!

Respond: Who needs to hear from you?

Day 342

Accept ● Forward ● Practice ●

Inspire: Today is Yours...

Today I will accomplish...

(fill in the blank)

You can, believe!

Respond: How will you accomplish it?

Day 343

Accept ● Forward ● Practice ●

Inspire: Layer Upon Layer...

This life is full of layers, and there's joy in each one, you just have to search for it sometimes! Don't get discouraged when it doesn't come easy. You can be encouraged by the fact that there's more to learn.

Respond: What does today's layer hold?

Day 344

Accept ● Forward ● Practice ●

Inspire: Say What?

What thoughts are occupying your mind? Think and say aloud positive thoughts and believe them! Your words and actions play a huge part in your success.

Respond: List some positives to say.

Day 345

Inspire: Treasure Map...

Map out on paper or computer that one big thing you've always wanted to do, and see what in it is doable right now. Then, do the doable now!

Respond: What's the first step?

Day 346

Accept ● Forward ● Practice ●

Inspire: Today is the Day...

See today for what it truly is... Yours to conquer! There's literally more than enough good for you to go after today, simply choose to see it and accept it.

Respond: What is today?

Day 347

Inspire: Question for You...

How much of what you look at on-line and on TV is helping you stay positive and focused on your dreams and goals? What we feed our senses feeds our beliefs and thought patterns. Nurture your soul with all you consume.

Respond: List some new options to watch.

Day 348

Accept ● Forward ● Practice ●

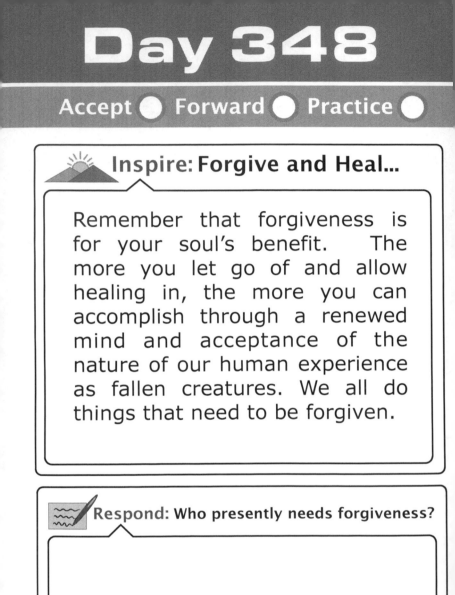

Inspire: Forgive and Heal...

Remember that forgiveness is for your soul's benefit. The more you let go of and allow healing in, the more you can accomplish through a renewed mind and acceptance of the nature of our human experience as fallen creatures. We all do things that need to be forgiven.

Respond: Who presently needs forgiveness?

Day 349

Accept ● Forward ● Practice ●

Inspire: Picture Perfect...

Take some time right now to focus on a picture in your mind of you succeeding. Then, begin to develop a daily pattern that allows that picture to stay in focus, no matter what the day brings. Your success matters to this life.

Respond: What does it look like?

Day 350

Accept ● Forward ● Practice ●

Inspire: Ready, Willing, Able...

Walk into every situation knowing you and your abilities are enough and will mean something to the end result.

Respond: Where do you make a difference?

Day 351

Accept ● Forward ● Practice ●

Inspire: Spread it Around...

If you haven't thought about it lately, think about success: in your life, in your work, and in your interaction with others. Not just for you, but for them as well. Make success contagious! It's a great thing to spread!

Respond: List some successful words.

Day 352

Accept ● Forward ● Practice ●

Inspire: Positively Impossible...

There are some things in life that seem impossible to be "positive" or upbeat about. I find most are from the past. If you're dealing with something like this, know that the past should never control us, but can be a learning tool for the future. You're free from it if you let yourself be.

Respond: What do you need to let go of?

Day 353

Accept ● Forward ● Practice ●

Inspire: You're Worthy...

Today, know that other people feel your worth, so feel it for yourself too!

Respond: What is awesome about you?

Day 354

Accept ● Forward ● Practice ●

Inspire: Reach & Stretch...

Everyday, stretch. Both physically and mentally, and find new strength in all parts of you. Now seriously, go stretch! It's good for you! Just be careful :)

Respond: Where can you stretch mentally?

Day 355

Accept ● Forward ● Practice ●

Inspire: Divine Dread...

If you're feeling a moment of dread, that just means you need to think of a moment of joy! Look at it as a reminder of the opposite and embrace the joyful thought instead!

Respond: List dread's replacements.

Day 356

Accept ● Forward ● Practice ●

Inspire: One Step Closer...

What's the one thing you have to do today you don't want to do? Do it first and celebrate the rest of your day! All the while saying, "Doing this moves me closer to my goals!"

Respond: What's achievable today?

Day 357

Accept ● Forward ● Practice ●

Inspire: Gotta Have Friends...

Make sure you have someone to talk to about life. Seek true friends and believe they will be there, then, be there for them too! An accountable friend is a necessity to a successful life.

Respond: Who are you accountable to?

Day 358

Accept ● Forward ● Practice ●

Inspire: Truth Be Told...

What do you need to tell the truth about that is just too hard to say? If it feels too big, practice it and talk it out with someone you can trust. Then, let it go and feel it's weight lift.

Respond: How does keeping it in feel?

Day 359

Accept ● Forward ● Practice ●

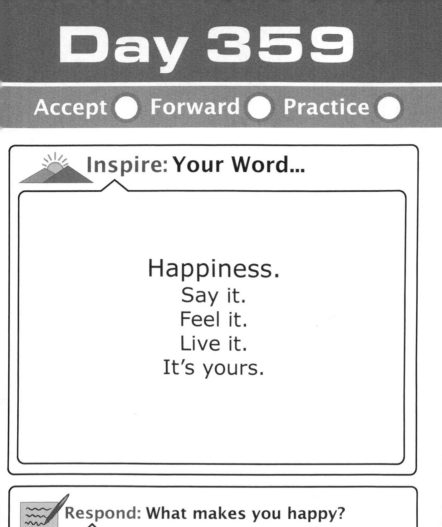

Inspire: Your Word...

Happiness.
Say it.
Feel it.
Live it.
It's yours.

Respond: What makes you happy?

Day 360

Accept ● Forward ● Practice ●

Inspire: It Does Matter...

Take a moment to go through in your head all the good in your life. It's all that good that gets us through when we feel bad. Keep the good at the forefront and feel success draw you in.

Respond: List the best of the best.

Day 361

Accept ● Forward ● Practice ●

Inspire: You Are Healthy...

Speak and believe health and vitality to yourself daily. You will feel the difference.

Respond: Write some healthy words.

Day 362

Accept ● Forward ● Practice ●

Inspire: Inspired Knowledge...

Know what inspires you, but just as importantly, what *doesn't*. Both matter in your growth. Knowledge breeds success!

Respond: What keeps you inspired?

Day 363

Accept ● Forward ● Practice ●

 Inspire: Life is Amazing...

Reflect today on all the wonderful people and things in your life, and feel encouraged! This is more than a good feeling, it is vital nutrients to your growth as someone unfazed by negativity.

Respond: Who and what gives you joy?

Day 364

Accept ● Forward ● Practice ●

Inspire: Truth is...

Life is filled with ups, downs, even sideways moments. It's all in how you handle them, and not letting them control your emotions. Life will happen to you, just be ready and stay focused on the positive. To worry is to waste time thinking about what you may never experience.

Respond: What can you lay aside?

Day 365

Accept ● Forward ● Practice ●

Inspire: Trust, Believe, Seek...

Without a belief in something greater than us, we often have trouble in life knowing exactly who and why we are here. I have found my life to be a gift from God. If you don't know where your life comes from, it's my prayer you'd seek to find out. God bless!

Respond: What is your belief system?

CONGRATULATIONS!

You've finished the book, and hopefully are feeling more inspired to pursue your dreams and simply have a more positive outlook on your day-to-day.

The next step for you is to remember that life will not always offer you the best, but that does not mean you cannot aspire and achieve the best for you and those around you. That "best" comes from not acquiring the most things, but having a belief system in place that no matter what you have, it is there to help you learn, achieve, and grow in your life. Everything from the simple act of getting up and brushing our teeth in the morning, to completing a life long goal matters in the daily health and betterment of you. All we encounter can be seen as tools for growth, or for beating us up, or becoming an obstacle.

You've probably heard it before, but it truly is all about perspective. Believe that life is not here to break you down and destroy you and your dreams; life is here to challenge you to become stronger, to grow, to gain wisdom and understanding from it's challenges. Life is a beautiful gift that if embraced will bring you joy, happiness, laughter, and yes, trials. But knowing that the trials are there to show you a new muscle that can grow into multiple muscles, multiple opportunities, and new adventures.

I believe in you, because you took the time to believe in yourself enough to go through this book, and at least do your best to change those parts that you feel need changing. If you've read through and applied even half of the days in this book, you have committed yourself to growth, and that will be honored by some form of fruit in your life. You are here to do great things! You are changing. You are are here to change your world, and perhaps the entire world, so keep pursuing and achieving.

While I hope this to be the first of many books I write, I would be remiss if I didn't give credit to those that have come before me and inspired me, my writing, and belief system. I highly recommend you read Dr. Norman Vincent Peale's works, and begin with his world renowned best seller, "The Power of Positive Thinking". That book changed my life and can change yours. I also recommend the works of Master Theologian C.S. Lewis. Beyond his children's books "The Chronicles of Narnia" Lewis' works include, "Mere Christianity", "The Screwtape Letters", "The Great Divorce", and my favorite, "The Problem of Pain" to name only a few. Both of these amazing authors give insight and perspective to the issues of mankind, and our constant yearning to know ourselves and God more.

It is my hope and prayer that you will go from this point with a new objective and outlook for your life from when you first began this book, and that some day I will feel and see the power and impact of your amazing life!

God bless, and many thanks!
James Arnold Taylor

Made in the USA
Middletown, DE
15 March 2015